Top Executive Compensation: 1989 Edition

*by Elizabeth R. Arreglado
and Charles A. Peck*

A Research Report from The Conference Board

Contents

Tables

ELECTRICAL AND ELECTRONIC MACHINERY

FABRICATED METAL PRODUCTS

FOOD AND KINDRED PRODUCTS

INDUSTRIAL CHEMICALS

MACHINERY (EXCEPT ELECTRICAL)

PAPER

Charts

From the President

1988 was a year of strong performance in most sectors of the U.S. economy. The 26th edition of The Conference Board's report on Top Executive Compensation reflects this relative prosperity. Executive bonuses, based on, and thus a measure of, corporate profitablility, were paid more often than in the prior year and, in half the industries covered, in larger amounts. The increase in bonus payments caused total current compensation to rise in all industries surveyed. Trends in total current compensation are presented by type of industry, as are bonus amounts paid by industry category, and trends in base salary. To aid companies in their salary planning, 1989 average salary increase budgets as well as projected average increase budgets for 1990 are shown.

For some time, companies have been aware of the need to tie top executive compensation to the long-term success of the enterprise, as well as to annual performance. Thus, most of the companies studied had at least one, and often more than one, long-term compensation plan. These include restricted stock awards, performance unit/share plans, and stock option plans. The report provides an in-depth analysis of the prevalence of these plans and the amounts of compensation realized through them.

The report continues its detailed coverage of total current compensation of the five highest-paid executives in companies in eight industry sectors: manufacturing, commercial banking, communications, diversified service, energy and natural resources, insurance, trade, and utilities. The data are presented so that a company can compare the pay of its five highest-paid executives with their counterparts in other industries or size categories.

For the second year, the report is presented in a format designed to ensure maximum clarity and ease of use. An introduction gives highlights and trends; a separate chapter deals with executive incentive compensation; and the remaining chapters are devoted to compensation paid within particular industries, and, in the case of manufacturing and insurance, within industry subgroups. The information presented in this report was obtained from several hundred companies. We thank the survey participants for the generous contribution of their time and effort. Without this contribution, the report would not have been possible.

PRESTON TOWNLEY
President

Highlights

The 1988 compensation of the five highest-paid executives in each of 643 surveyed companies in eight major types of businesses is analyzed in this report. The major focus is on 1988 total current compensation, defined as base salary paid in 1988 and bonus earned for 1988 company performance. Using this report, a company can compare the 1988 compensation of its top-paid executives with that of their counterparts in companies of similar size and type of business.

The report also describes the incidence of, and trends in, four important elements of the executive compensation package: annual bonus plans, long-term performance plans, stock option plans, and restricted stock plans. For stock options, the size of option grants during 1988 is shown, as well as the net gain for options exercised during 1988. For restricted stock plans, the size of grants during 1988 is reported. The size of payouts during 1988 is given for long-term performance plans, and the size of contingent awards made under these plans during the year is also reported.

Pay Trends

Compared with 1987, 1988 total current compensation was higher in all the industry categories surveyed. Total current compensation increased 20.3 percent in energy and natural resources, 15.5 percent in commercial banking, 12.9 percent in manufacturing, 8.2 percent in insurance and utilities, 4.5 percent in trade, and 3.2 percent in diversified service.

Salaries rose in 1988 in each type of business. The increase was 10.2 percent in commercial banking, 10.0 percent in manufacturing, 8.3 percent in insurance and utilities, 7.4 percent in trade, 6.2 percent in energy and natural resources, and 5.4 percent in diversified service. There were insufficient data to show a pay trend for communications.

Estimates of salary increase budgets made in April and May 1989 for all salaried employees show a median increase of 5.0 percent for nonexempts and exempts, and 5.5 percent for executives for 1989. The projection for 1990 is the same for all three categories.

Annual Bonus Plans

Annual bonuses are virtually universal in manufacturing, diversified service, energy and natural resources, and commercial banks. Bonuses are very widely used in communications and trade, with 89 percent of the companies in each industry reporting them, as well as among insurance companies, where 86 percent have bonus plans. They are least often found in utilities where only 68 percent have plans. However, there is a definite trend toward the adoption of bonus plans in the utilities industry; five years ago only 37 percent of the companies reported such plans.

The size of the median bonus award for the CEO, as a percentage of salary, is lowest in utilities and insurance, 36 and 38 percent, respectively. Trade and commercial banking show very similar patterns at 45 and 47 percent, respectively. Communications and diversified service both had median CEO bonuses of 50 percent. Energy companies paid a median bonus of 64 percent, while manufacturing was the high payer at 69 percent.

Restricted Stock Plans

Under these plans, companies make outright awards of restricted shares, which are often subject to forfeiture until they are "earned out" over a stipulated period of continued employment. A significant minority of companies in each type of business have a plan for awards of restricted stock to top executives: energy and stock insurance companies, 41 percent, banks, 38 percent, trade, 35 percent, diversified service and manufacturing, 34 percent, communications, 28 percent, and utilities, 17 percent.

During 1988, the median award to the five highest-paid executives as a group ranged from a high of 102 percent of salary in diversified service to a low of 38 percent in banks and stock insurance companies.

Long-Term Performance Plans

A minority of companies in each industry group have long-term performance plans. Top executives are given a contingent award of shares or units at the beginning of a performance period; the payment of these awards is determined by how closely specified corporate financial targets are met during a three-, four-, or five-year performance period. Such plans are most prevalent in communications, 44 percent, manufacturing, 34 percent, and energy, 32 percent. Thirty-one percent of the surveyed trade companies have long-term performance plans, as do 28 percent of the insurance companies. Long-term plans are least often found in diversified service and utilities (27 percent) and commercial banking (25 percent).

During 1988, the median *award* to the five highest-paid executives as a group ranged from 57 percent of salary in energy and natural resources to 25 percent in commercial banking. The median *payment* for 1988 ranged from 60 percent of salary among manufacturers to 20 percent in banking.

Stock Option Plans

The majority of companies in all industry categories have stock option plans, except for utilities where only 38 percent have them. Eighty-four percent of the surveyed manufacturing companies have them, as do 83 percent of the communications companies, 78 percent of the energy companies, 77 percent of trade, 74 percent of the banks, 70 percent of diversified service, and 68 percent of the stock insurance companies.

The median stock option grant made in 1988 to the five highest-paid executives as a group ranged from the equivalent of 94 to 167 percent of base salary, depending on the type of business. The median net gain for options exercised during 1988 ranged from a high of 117 percent of salary in energy firms to a low of 21 percent in trade.

Method

Information for this report was collected during April and May 1989. Questionnaires were mailed to 2,737 U.S. companies. Those surveyed were the large manufacturers (sales of approximately $100 million or more) and companies of comparable size in seven other industry categories. The survey information was supplemented with publicly available data from corporate reports.

Usable information was collected from 643 companies in eight industry categories. The 643 companies were distributed by industry category as follows:

Manufacturing companies (321)
Gas, electric, water, and telecommunications (71)
Commercial banks (68)
Health, life and property and casualty insurance companies (58)
Diversified service companies, including computer services, health care, hotel/restaurant/entertainment, real estate and transportation (44)
Energy and natural resources companies (37)
Wholesale and retail trade companies (26)
Communications companies, including broadcasting and printing and publishing (18)

Authors' Acknowledgment

Analytical programming was provided by Robert Vidal under the direction of E. Kay Worrell, Director, Records and Research Support. Charts were prepared under the direction of Chuck N. Tow, Chief Chartist.

Chapter 1
Introduction

This report is primarily an analysis of the 1988 compensation of the five highest-paid executives in each of 643 companies (see box on "Method"). The major emphasis is on base salary *paid* in 1988 and the bonus *earned* for 1988 company performance, regardless of when paid. Total current compensation is the sum of the two. The report also describes the prevalence of and trends in four major forms of executive incentive compensation: annual bonus plans, restricted stock plans, long-term performance plans, and stock option plans.

Pay Trends

The change in CEO total current compensation from 1987 to 1988 is given in Table 1 below. This is the median change for the position in those companies that furnished data in both years. The individuals in the CEO positions were not necessarily the same in both years. The same information with respect to salary is shown in Table 2.

Table 1: CEO Total Current Compensation Change, 1988 over 1987

Industry Category*	Number of Companies	Median Change
Energy	20	20.3%
Commercial banking	27	15.5
Manufacturing	130	12.9
Insurance	38	8.2
Utilities	47	8.2
Trade	11	4.5
Diversified service	21	3.2

*Insufficient data for Communications.

Table 2: CEO Salary Change, 1988 over 1987

Industry Category*	Number of Companies	Median Change
Commercial banking	27	10.2%
Manufacturing	130	10.0
Insurance	38	8.3
Utilities	47	8.3
Trade	11	7.4
Energy	20	6.2
Diversified service	21	5.4

*Insufficient data for Communications.

As an indicator of future salary increases, companies were asked during April and May 1989 to provide the 1989 salary increase budget and the 1990 anticipated salary increase budget for their executive, exempt, and nonexempt populations. The results are shown in Table 3 for all industries as a group and separately for those industries for which the data were sufficient to allow individual analysis.

Table 3: Salary Increase Budgets, 1989 and 1990

	1989		Estimated for 1990	
Type of Business	Number of Companies*	Median	Number of Companies*	Median
ALL INDUSTRIES				
Nonexempt	468	5.0%	329	5.0%
Exempt	490	5.0	342	5.0
Executive	474	5.5	332	5.5
COMMERCIAL BANKING				
Nonexempt	65	5.2	42	5.0
Exempt	65	5.5	42	5.5
Executive	63	5.5	41	5.5
DIVERSIFIED SERVICE				
Nonexempt	30	5.3	24	5.0
Exempt	30	5.4	24	5.4
Executive	29	6.0	24	5.5
INSURANCE				
Nonexempt	54	5.5	35	5.5
Exempt	54	5.5	35	5.5
Executive	50	5.5	34	5.7
MANUFACTURING				
Nonexempt	192	5.0	137	5.0
Exempt	198	5.0	143	5.2
Executive	196	5.5	140	5.5
UTILITIES				
Nonexempt	54	4.5	42	4.5
Exempt	64	5.0	46	5.0
Executive	60	5.0	44	5.0

* Other industry groups are included in totals but not shown separately because of small samples.

Chapter 2
Executive Incentive Compensation

This chapter examines the four major forms of executive incentive compensation, which are defined as follows:

Annual Bonus: Generally, a percentage of profits is used to create a fund that is apportioned among the eligible executives based on individual contributions to profitability.

Restricted Stock: Shares of company stock are awarded to executives and are subject to restrictions as to sale or transfer, usually for three to five years. Additional restrictions often call for forfeiture if the executive terminates employment during the restricted period.

Long-Term Performance Plans: Under these plans executives are awarded contingent grants of cash (long-term performance *units*) or stock (long-term performance *shares*). The payment of the award usually depends on the achievement of three-to-five-year financial performance goals.

Stock Options: These arrangements provide executives a right to purchase shares of company stock at a fixed price over a stated period of time. "Incentive stock options" (ISOs) meet Internal Revenue Code requirements, while "nonqualified stock options" do not. An option plan may allow "stock swaps" where previously acquired shares are used to exercise an option. "Stock appreciation rights" (SARs) may be attached to stock options. The SAR gives an optionee, in lieu of exercising the stock option, the right to receive an amount equal to the appreciation in the stock price since the date of grant.

To indicate trends in the incidence of these plans, the number reported in the 1989 survey is compared with the number reported in the 1984 survey. A five-year span is believed to be a good indicator of such trends. It should be noted that while the companies in the two surveys are not identical, the sample is relatively constant.

Table 4: Prevalence of Annual Bonus Plans

Industry Category	Total Companies	May, 1989 With Bonus Plan Number	May, 1989 With Bonus Plan Percent	May, 1984 Percent With Bonus Plan
Manufacturing	321	318	99%	92%
Diversified service	44	43	98	*
Energy	37	36	97	*
Commercial banking	68	64	94	73
Communications	18	16	89	*
Trade	26	23	89	78
Insurance	58	50	86	64
Utilities	71	48	68	37

* Data not available.

Table 5: Prevalence of Bonus Awards

Industry Category	Total Responses	Percent that Paid Bonus 1988	Percent that Paid Bonus 1987
Diversified service	40	100%	93%
Insurance	45	98	91
Commercial banking	52	98	87
Manufacturing	189	97	96
Energy	25	96	84
Trade	22	96	100
Utilities	42	95	86
Communications	9	89	100

Table 6: Median CEO Bonus Awards for 1988

Industry Category	Number of CEOS	Percent of Salary
Manufacturing	180	69%
Energy	24	64
Communications	6	50
Diversified service	38	50
Commercial banking	51	47
Trade	22	45
Insurance	44	38
Utilities	43	36

Table 7: Prevalence of Restricted Stock Plans

		May, 1989		May, 1984
		With Restricted Stock		Percent with
Industry Category	Total Companies	Number	Percent	Restricted Stock
Energy	37	15	41%	*
Insurance: stock	22	9	41	15%
Commercial banking . . .	68	26	38	12
Trade	26	9	35	21
Diversified service	44	15	34	*
Manufacturing	321	109	34	21
Communications	18	5	28	*
Utilities	71	12	17	6

* Data not available.

Table 8: Median Restricted Stock Awards for 1988 to The Five Highest-Paid Executives as a Group

Industry Category*	Number of Companies	Number of Executives	Median (Percent of Salary)
Diversified service	6	20	102%
Energy	5	18	59
Utilities	6	23	58
Manufacturing	39	160	47
Commercial banking	12	48	38
Insurance: stock	8	27	38

* Insufficient data for industries not shown.

Table 9: Prevalence of Long-Term Performance Plans

		May, 1989		May, 1984
		With Long-term Performance Plans		Percent with Long-term
Industry Category	Total Companies	Number	Percent	Performance Plans
Communications	18	8	44%	*
Manufacturing	321	109	34	35%
Energy	37	12	32	*
Trade	26	8	31	18
Insurance	58	16	28	20
Diversified service	44	12	27	*
Utilities	71	19	27	12
Commercial banking . . .	68	17	25	19

* Data not available.

Table 10: Types of Long-Term Performance Plans

		Number and Percent of Plans by Type					
		Both Unit and Share Plans		Only Unit Plan		Only Share Plan	
Industry Category	Total Plans	Number	Percent	Number	Percent	Number	Percent
Manufacturing	109	8	7%	64	59%	37	34%
Utilities	19	—	—	4	21	15	79
Commercial banking	17	1	6	11	65	5	29
Insurance	16	—	—	11	69	5	31
Diversified service .	12	—	—	8	67	4	33
Energy	12	—	—	9	75	3	25
Communications . . .	8	—	—	5	63	3	38
Trade	8	1	13	5	63	2	25

Table 11: Median Long-Term Performance Awards for 1988 To The Five Highest-Paid Executives as a Group

Industry Category*	Number of Companies	Number of Executives	Median (Percent of Salary)
Energy	7	33	57%
Manufacturing	51	241	55
Utilities	12	53	52
Diversified service	5	23	44
Insurance	10	45	39
Commercial banking	11	52	25

* Insufficient data for industries not shown.

Table 12: Median Long-Term Performance Payments for 1988 To the Five Highest-Paid Executives as a Group

Industry Category*	Number of Companies	Number of Executives	Median (Percent of Salary)
Manufacturing	33	136	60%
Diversified service	5	23	53
Trade	6	22	46
Utilities	12	56	42
Energy	9	37	40
Insurance	10	40	29
Commercial banking.......	4	16	20

* Insufficient data for Communications.

Table 13: Prevalence of Stock Option Plans

Industry Category	Total Companies	May, 1989 With Stock Option Plan Number	May, 1989 With Stock Option Plan Percent	May, 1984 Percent with Stock Option Plan
Manufacturing..........	321	270	84%	84%
Communications	18	15	83	*
Energy................	37	29	78	*
Trade.................	26	20	77	77
Commercial banking.....	68	50	74	50
Diversified service......	44	31	70	*
Insurance: stock	22	15	68	43
Utilities	71	27	38	20

*Data not available.

Table 14: Types of Options

Industry Category	Total Responses	Both ISO and Nonqualified Number	Both ISO and Nonqualified Percent	Only ISO Number	Only ISO Percent	Only Nonqualified Number	Only Nonqualified Percent
Manufacturing	251	208	83%	7	3%	36	14%
Commercial banking	42	37	88	4	10	1	2
Diversified service ..	26	22	85	2	8	2	8
Utilities	26	20	77	—	—	6	23
Energy	24	18	75	—	—	6	25
Trade.............	19	16	84	—	—	3	16
Communications ...	14	12	86	1	7	1	7
Insurance: stock....	13	9	69	1	8	3	23

Table 15: 1988 Stock Option Grants

Industry Category	Companies with Stock Option Plan	Granted Options in 1988 Number	Granted Options in 1988 Percent
Insurance: stock	15	14	93%
Diversified service	31	27	87
Manufacturing	270	220	82
Commercial banking	50	40	80
Energy	29	23	79
Trade.....................	20	15	75
Utilities	27	19	70
Communications	15	10	67

Table 16: 1988 Stock Option Grants by Type

Industry Category*	Total Responses	Both ISO and Nonqualifed Number	Both ISO and Nonqualifed Percent	ISO Only Number	ISO Only Percent	Nonqualified Only Number	Nonqualified Only Percent
Manufacturing	74	19	26%	10	14%	45	61%
Commercial banking	22	9	41	7	32	6	27
Diversified service	16	2	13	3	19	11	69
Utilities...........................	14	2	14	1	7	11	79
Energy	8	3	38	2	25	3	38
Trade..............................	8	—	—	—	—	8	100
Insurance: stock	6	3	50	—	—	3	50

*Insufficent data for Communications.

Table 17: Incentive Stock Options with Stock Swap— Stock Appreciation Rights

Industry Category	ISO Plans	With Stock Swap		With SAR	
		Number	Percent	Number	Percent
Manufacturing	215	86	40%	63	29%
Commercial banking	41	21	51	15	37
Diversified service . .	24	20	83	13	54
Utilities	20	12	60	10	50
Energy	18	11	61	11	61
Trade	16	13	81	5	31
Communications . . .	13	3	23	4	31
Insurance: stock . . .	10	5	50	7	70

Table 18: Nonqualified Options with Stock Swap— Stock Appreciation Rights

Industry Category	Nonqualified Options	With Stock Swap		With SAR	
		Number	Percent	Number	Percent
Manufacturing	244	91	37%	68	28%
Commercial banking .	38	20	53	15	40
Utilities	26	16	62	13	50
Diversified service . . .	24	20	83	13	54
Energy	24	13	54	15	63
Trade	19	15	79	6	32
Communications	13	3	23	4	31
Insurance: stock	12	6	50	7	58

Table 19: Size of 1988 Stock Option Grants To The Five Highest-Paid Executives as a Group

Industry Category*	Number of Companies	Number of Executives	Size of Grant (Percent of Salary)		
			Median	Middle 50% Range	
				Low	High
Diversified service	21	97	167%	93%	321%
Trade	13	59	159	61	237
Energy	19	88	124	69	241
Manufacturing	125	578	117	71	208
Utilities	18	88	105	71	189
Insurance: stock	14	62	96	53	128
Commercial banking . . .	36	159	94	60	151

*Insufficent data for Communications.

Table 20: Gains at Exercise in 1988 of the Five Highest-Paid Executives as a Group

Industry Category*	Number of Companies	Number of Executives	Dollars			Percent of Salary		
			Median	Middle 50% Range		Median	Middle 50% Range	
				Low	High		Low	High
Energy	9	24	$370,000	$142,000	$905,000	117%	32%	214%
Commercial banking.	20	57	174,000	92,000	317,000	58	31	95
Manufacturing	66	191	160,000	58,000	498,000	49	24	128
Trade	6	19	101,000	13,000	666,000	21	4	62
Diversified service	16	48	71,000	35,000	382,000	45	11	117
Utilties.	10	24	54,000	29,000	128,000	22	10	44

* Insufficient data for industries not shown.

Chapter 3
Compensation by Industry Category

The balance of the report contains the information listed below for each of the eight major industry categories and for 12 manufacturing subcategories.

- Distribution of companies according to size;
- Median and low and high of middle 50 percent range for total current compensation and salary;
- Regression formulas for total current compensation and salary;
- Charts showing regression lines measuring the relationship between total current compensation and company size; and
- Total current compensation and salary of the second through fifth highest-paid executives as a percentage of CEO's (highest paid) pay.

With the exception of communications, where data were insufficient for analysis, each major industry section also contains an analysis relating bonus awards to company size and a table showing the size of bonus awards for each of the five executives. Life insurance and property and casualty insurance are analyzed in separate sections.

Executive Pay and Company Size

The regression line charts and the regression formulas are based on the generally accepted belief that there is a cause-and-effect relationship between company size and executive pay. The CEO of a large company is paid more than the CEO of a small company because the large company CEO has a more difficult and demanding job.

The regression lines on the charts measure the general relationship between total current compensation and company size. The lines can be used for determining the average compensation of executives for any company size. For greater precision, the regression formulas can be used. (See the Appendix for an explanation of how to use the formulas.)

Chapter 4
Manufacturing

Chart 1: Total Current Compensation of the Five Highest-Paid Executives, by Company Sales

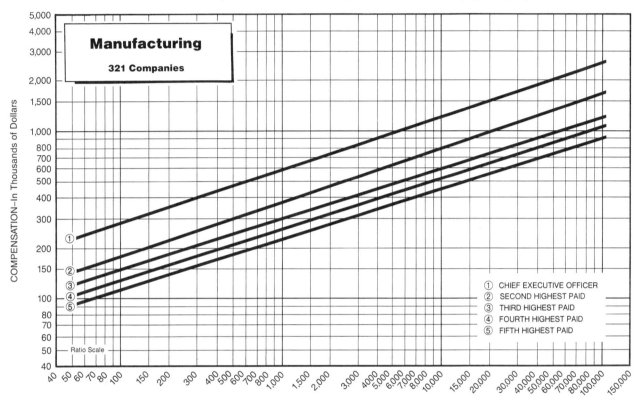

SALES–In Millions of Dollars

Table 21: 1988 Sales Volume

1988 Sales	Companies	
	Number	Percent
$5 billion and over	61	19%
2-4,999 billion	57	18
1-1,999 billion	51	16
500-999 million	55	17
300-499 million	33	10
200-299 million	32	10
199 million and under	32	10
TOTAL	321	100%

Median	Middle 50% Range	
	Low	High
$1.1 billion	$388 million	$3.5 billion

Table 22: 1988 Total Current Compensation

Compensation Rank	Median	Middle 50% Range	
		Low	High
CEO	$654,000	$412,000	$957,000
Second highest	405,000	253,000	611,000
Third highest	320,000	214,000	459,000
Fourth highest	278,000	182,000	417,000
Fifth highest	253,000	165,000	365,000

Table 23: 1988 Total Current Compensation Regression Formula

Compensation Rank	Formula	r^2
CEO	$\log Y = 1.8080 + 0.3210 \log X$	61%
Second highest	$\log Y = 1.6380 + 0.3120 \log X$	64
Third highest	$\log Y = 1.5890 + 0.2960 \log X$	65
Fourth highest	$\log Y = 1.4930 + 0.3060 \log X$	69
Fifth highest	$\log Y = 1.4540 + 0.3010 \log X$	66

Table 24: Total Current Compensation as a Percentage of CEO's Total Current Compensation*

Compensation Rank	Median	Middle 50% Range Low	Middle 50% Range High
Second highest	66%	54%	77%
Third highest	50	42	60
Fourth highest	43	37	51
Fifth highest	39	33	46

* Please note that for all tables showing this relationship, the percentages are not based on the preceding table showing the median and the middle 50 percent range of total current compensation.

Table 25: 1988 Salary

Compensation Rank	Median	Middle 50% Range Low	Middle 50% Range High
CEO	$435,000	$300,000	$585,000
Second highest	260,000	199,000	398,000
Third highest	217,000	160,000	295,000
Fourth highest	195,000	145,000	261,000
Fifth highest	184,000	130,000	237,000

Table 26: 1988 Salary Regression Formula

Compensation Rank	Formula	r^2
CEO	$\log Y = 1.8920 + 0.2340 \log X$	55%
Second highest	$\log Y = 1.6510 + 0.2490 \log X$	57
Third highest	$\log Y = 1.6220 + 0.2300 \log X$	56
Fourth highest	$\log Y = 1.5530 + 0.2350 \log X$	63
Fifth highest	$\log Y = 1.5310 + 0.2290 \log X$	58

Table 27: Salary as a Percentage of CEO's Salary*

Compensation Rank	Median	Middle 50% Range Low	Middle 50% Range High
Second highest	65%	56%	77%
Third highest	53	46	59
Fourth highest	46	41	53
Fifth highest	42	37	48

* Please note that for all tables showing this relationship, the percentages are not based on the preceding table showing the median and middle 50 percent range of salary.

Table 28: 1988 Bonus Awards (as Percent of Salary), by Company Size

Executive	Sales Volume Middle 50% Range Low $388 Million	Sales Volume Middle 50% Range Median $1.1 Billion	Sales Volume Middle 50% Range High $3.5 Billion
CEO			
1988 Bonus	51%	62%	75%
Salary	$300,000	$386,000	$511,000
Second Highest			
1988 Bonus	48%	58%	69%
Salary	$187,000	$245,000	$332,000
Third Highest			
1988 Bonus	45%	54%	65%
Salary	$158,000	$202,000	$266,000
Fourth Highest			
1988 Bonus	39%	49%	61%
Salary	$139,000	$179,000	$237,000
Fifth Highest			
1988 Bonus	34%	45%	58%
Salary	$128,000	$163,000	$214,000

Table 29: 1988 Bonus Awards

1988 Bonus Awards (Percent of Salary)	CEOS		Second Highest Paid		Third Highest Paid		Fourth Highest Paid		Fifth Highest Paid	
	Number	Percent	Number	Percent	Number	Percent	Number	Percent	Number	Percent
100% or more	39	22%	31	17%	26	14%	16	9%	12	7%
90-99	11	6	8	4	8	4	12	6	8	4
80-89	21	12	12	6	8	4	7	4	6	3
70-79	18	10	17	9	24	13	18	10	13	7
60-69	21	12	25	13	16	9	19	10	24	13
50-59	17	9	36	19	26	14	25	13	24	13
40-49	24	13	15	8	25	13	37	20	26	14
30-39	14	8	21	11	26	14	24	13	19	10
20-29	7	4	13	7	20	11	19	10	33	18
10-19	4	2	7	4	6	3	7	4	15	8
Less than 10%	4	2	2	1	2	1	4	2	3	2
Total	180	100%	187	100%	187	100%	188	100%	183	100%
Median Bonus	69%		59%		55%		50%		47%	
Middle 50% Range	47 – 93%		41 – 81%		36 – 76%		37 – 72%		28 – 66%	

Aerospace

Chart 2: Total Current Compensation of the Five Highest-Paid Executives, by Company Sales

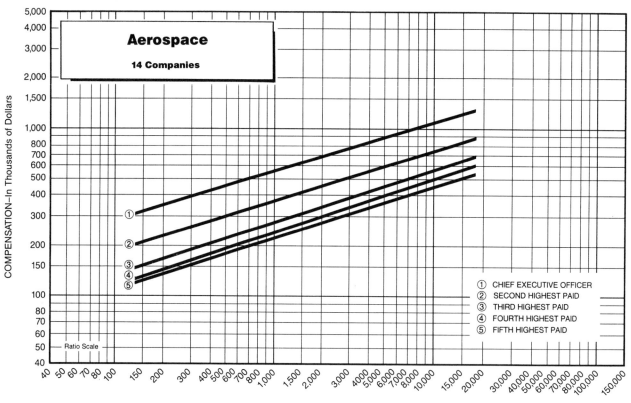

SALES–In Millions of Dollars

Table 30: 1988 Sales Volume

1988 Sales	Companies	
	Number	Percent
$5 billion and over	8	57%
2-4,999 billion	3	21
1-1,999 billion	—	—
500-999 million	1	7
300-499 million	2	14
Total	14	100%

Median	Middle 50% Range	
	Low	High
$5.7 billion	$2.3 billion	$11.9 billion

Table 31: 1988 Total Current Compensation

Compensation Rank	Median	Middle 50% Range	
		Low	High
CEO	$875,000	$666,000	$1,180,000
Second highest	633,000	470,000	810,000
Third highest	447,000	285,000	618,000
Fourth highest	380,000	285,000	477,000
Fifth highest	350,000	260,000	441,000

Table 32: 1988 Total Current Compensation Regression Formula

Compensation Rank	Formula	r^2
CEO	$\log Y = 1.8660 + 0.2930 \log X$	64%
Second highest	$\log Y = 1.6250 + 0.3110 \log X$	76
Third highest	$\log Y = 1.4940 + 0.3140 \log X$	81
Fourth highest	$\log Y = 1.4370 + 0.3150 \log X$	85
Fifth highest	$\log Y = 1.4440 + 0.3010 \log X$	85

Table 33: Total Current Compensation as a Percentage of CEO's Total Current Compensation

Compensation Rank	Median	Middle 50% Range	
		Low	High
Second highest	69%	66%	77%
Third highest	51	43	61
Fourth highest	45	37	52
Fifth highest	38	37	47

Table 34: 1988 Salary

Compensation Rank	Median	Middle 50% Range	
		Low	High
CEO	$545,000	$375,000	$730,000
Second highest	440,000	293,000	450,000
Third highest	265,000	210,000	440,000
Fourth highest	260,000	210,000	375,000
Fifth highest	240,000	190,000	295,000

Table 35: 1988 Salary Regression Formula

Compensation Rank	Formula	r^2
CEO	$\log Y = 2.0730 + 0.1750 \log X$	41%
Second highest	$\log Y = 2.0500 + 0.1450 \log X$	42
Third highest	$\log Y = 1.6240 + 0.2260 \log X$	66
Fourth highest	$\log Y = 1.5880 + 0.2230 \log X$	75
Fifth highest	$\log Y = 1.6510 + 0.1930 \log X$	76

Table 36: Salary as a Percentage of CEO's Salary

Compensation Rank	Median	Middle 50% Range	
		Low	High
Second highest	78%	62%	84%
Third highest	56	47	60
Fourth highest	48	45	59
Fifth highest	43	36	54

Computer Hardware and Office Equipment

Chart 3: Total Current Compensation of the Five Highest-Paid Executives, by Company Sales

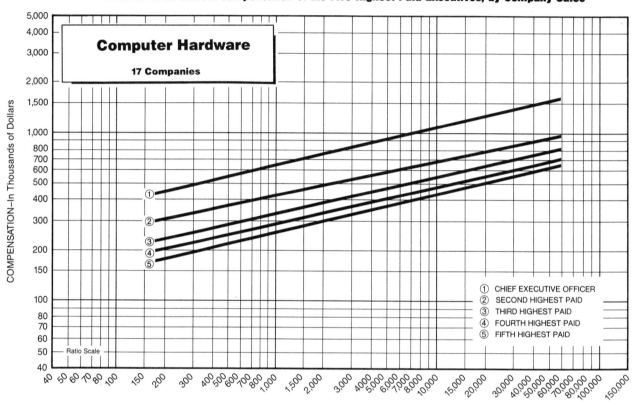

SALES–In Millions of Dollars

Table 37: 1988 Sales Volume

1988 Sales	Companies	
	Number	Percent
$5 billion and over	6	35%
2-4,999 billion	1	6
1-1,999 billion	2	12
500-999 million	3	18
300-499 million	1	6
200-299 million	2	12
199 million and under	2	12
Total	17	100%

Median	Middle 50% Range	
	Low	High
$1.2 billion	$439 million	$9.8 billion

Table 38: 1988 Total Current Compensation

Compensation Rank	Median	Middle 50% Range	
		Low	High
CEO	$662,000	$499,000	$1,157,000
Second highest	466,000	304,000	797,000
Third highest	327,000	238,000	608,000
Fourth highest	310,000	195,000	503,000
Fifth highest	270,000	182,000	451,000

Table 39: 1988 Total Current Compensation Regression Formula

Compensation Rank	Formula	r^2
CEO	log Y = 2.1340 + 0.2240 log X	52%
Second highest	log Y = 2.0170 + 0.2040 log X	46
Third highest	log Y = 1.8840 + 0.2130 log X	48
Fourth highest	log Y = 1.8040 + 0.2180 log X	50
Fifth highest	log Y = 1.7310 + 0.2250 log X	53

Table 40: Total Current Compensation as a Percentage of CEO's Total Current Compensation

Compensation Rank	Median	Middle 50% Range	
		Low	High
Second highest	66%	56%	77%
Third highest	51	43	59
Fourth highest	47	39	50
Fifth highest	40	35	45

Table 41: 1988 Salary

Compensation Rank	Median	Middle 50% Range	
		Low	High
CEO	$510,000	$353,000	$600,000
Second highest	282,000	172,000	398,000
Third highest	250,000	210,000	349,000
Fourth highest	261,000	180,000	298,000
Fifth highest	211,000	165,000	281,000

Table 42: 1988 Salary Regression Formula

Compensation Rank	Formula	r^2
CEO	log Y = 2.1880 + 0.1540 log X	56%
Second highest	log Y = 1.9210 + 0.1690 log X	39
Third highest	log Y = 1.9180 + 0.1570 log X	66
Fourth highest	log Y = 1.8230 + 0.1730 log X	62
Fifth highest	log Y = 1.7150 + 0.1890 log X	65

Table 43: Salary as a Percentage of CEO's Salary

Compensation Rank	Median	Middle 50% Range	
		Low	High
Second highest	57%	47%	72%
Third highest	54	47	71
Fourth highest	47	43	54
Fifth highest	40	37	58

Consumer Chemicals

Chart 4: Total Current Compensation of the Five Highest-Paid Executives, by Company Sales

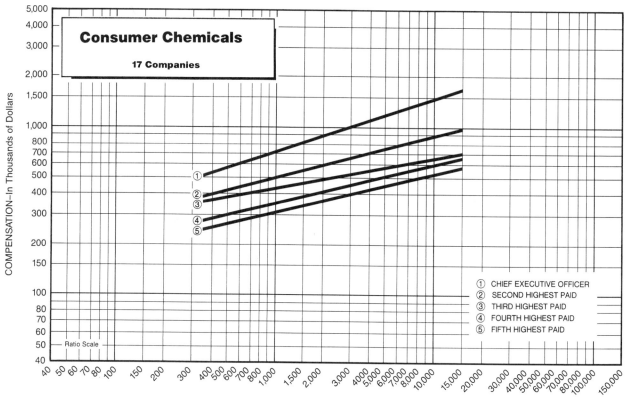

Consumer Chemicals

17 Companies

COMPENSATION–In Thousands of Dollars

Ratio Scale

① CHIEF EXECUTIVE OFFICER
② SECOND HIGHEST PAID
③ THIRD HIGHEST PAID
④ FOURTH HIGHEST PAID
⑤ FIFTH HIGHEST PAID

SALES–In Millions of Dollars

Table 44: 1988 Sales Volume

1988 Sales	Companies	
	Number	Percent
$5 billion and over	4	24%
2-4,999 billion	7	41
1-1,999 billion	1	6
500-999 million	3	18
300-499 million	2	12
200-299 million	—	—
199 million and under	—	—
Total	17	100%

Median	Middle 50% Range	
	Low	High
$3.9 billion	$943 million	$4.9 billion

Table 45: 1988 Total Current Compensation

Compensation Rank	Median	Middle 50% Range	
		Low	High
CEO	$1,000,000	$770,000	$1,250,000
Second highest	652,000	458,000	800,000
Third highest	529,000	371,000	634,000
Fourth highest	483,000	319,000	529,000
Fifth highest	368,000	313,000	485,000

Table 46: 1988 Total Current Compensation Regression Formula

Compensation Rank	Formula	r^2
CEO	log Y = 1.9060 + 0.3160 log X	53%
Second highest	log Y = 1.9800 + 0.2380 log X	44
Third highest	log Y = 2.1490 + 0.1630 log X	24
Fourth highest	log Y = 1.8750 + 0.2230 log X	48
Fifth highest	log Y = 1.8220 + 0.2230 log X	49

Table 47: Total Current Compensation as a Percentage of CEO's Total Current Compensation

Compensation Rank	Median	Middle 50% Range	
		Low	High
Second highest	62%	52%	81%
Third highest	48	44	57
Fourth highest	40	38	51
Fifth highest	38	35	48

Table 48: 1988 Salary

Compensation Rank	Median	Middle 50% Range	
		Low	High
CEO	$642,000	$500,000	$750,000
Second highest	422,000	275,000	458,000
Third highest	335,000	245,000	408,000
Fourth highest	296,000	225,000	369,000
Fifth highest	226,000	195,000	340,000

Table 49: 1988 Salary Regression Formula

Compensation Rank	Formula	r^2
CEO	log Y = 1.9710 + 0.2350 log X	38%
Second highest	log Y = 1.8050 + 0.2330 log X	53
Third highest	log Y = 1.9660 + 0.1610 log X	35
Fourth highest	log Y = 1.8930 + 0.1660 log X	34
Fifth highest	log Y = 1.7730 + 0.1860 log X	37

Table 50: Salary as a Percentage of CEO's Salary

Compensation Rank	Median	Middle 50% Range	
		Low	High
Second highest	66%	58%	80%
Third highest	51	46	58
Fourth highest	46	40	51
Fifth highest	41	38	50

Electrical and Electronic Machinery

Chart 5: Total Current Compensation of the Five Highest-Paid Executives, by Company Sales

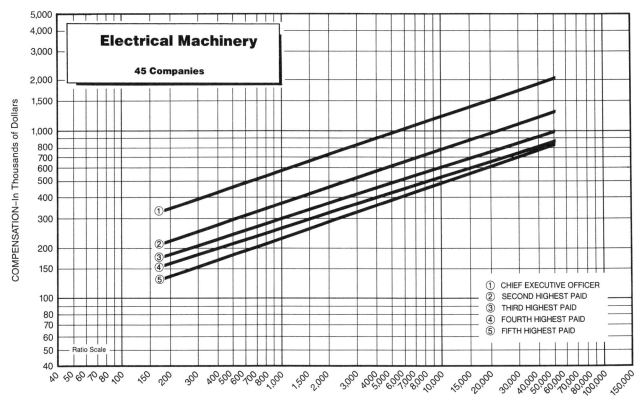

SALES–In Millions of Dollars

Table 51: 1988 Sales Volume

1988 Sales	Companies	
	Number	Percent
$5 billion and over	7	16%
2-4,999 billion	7	16
1-1,999 billion	7	16
500-999 million	7	16
300-499 million	2	4
200-299 million	8	18
199 million and under	7	16
Total	45	100%

Median	Middle 50% Range	
	Low	High
$774 million	$260 million	$2.3 billion

Table 52: 1988 Total Current Compensation

Compensation Rank	Median	Middle 50% Range	
		Low	High
CEO	$563,000	$390,000	$798,000
Second highest	331,000	224,000	520,000
Third highest	294,000	189,000	393,000
Fourth highest	260,000	163,000	336,000
Fifth highest	216,000	147,000	320,000

Table 53: 1988 Total Current Compensation Regression Formula

Compensation Rank	Formula	r^2
CEO	log Y = 1.8140 + 0.3170 log X	59%
Second highest	log Y = 1.6190 + 0.3170 log X	68
Third highest	log Y = 1.5780 + 0.3000 log X	74
Fourth highest	log Y = 1.5220 + 0.2980 log X	79
Fifth highest	log Y = 1.4010 + 0.3190 log X	77

Table 54: Total Current Compensation as a Percentage of CEO's Total Current Compensation

Compensation Rank	Median	Middle 50% Range	
		Low	High
Second highest	67%	52%	77%
Third highest	48	42	63
Fourth highest	42	37	53
Fifth highest	40	31	44

Table 55: 1988 Salary

Compensation Rank	Median	Middle 50% Range	
		Low	High
CEO	$420,000	$294,000	$563,000
Second highest	245,000	200,000	429,000
Third highest	222,000	176,000	292,000
Fourth highest	188,000	139,000	262,000
Fifth highest	180,000	130,000	250,000

Table 56: 1988 Salary Regression Formula

Compensation Rank	Formula	r^2
CEO	log Y = 1.9120 + 0.2270 log X	52%
Second highest	log Y = 1.6780 + 0.2440 log X	52
Third highest	log Y = 1.7360 + 0.2020 log X	50
Fourth highest	log Y = 1.6860 + 0.1930 log X	57
Fifth highest	log Y = 1.5840 + 0.2170 log X	68

Table 57: Salary as a Percentage of CEO's Salary

Compensation Rank	Median	Middle 50% Range	
		Low	High
Second highest	65%	52%	80%
Third highest	55	43	63
Fourth highest	47	38	55
Fifth highest	42	38	47

Fabricated Metal Products

Chart 6: Total Current Compensation of the Five Highest-Paid Executives, by Company Sales

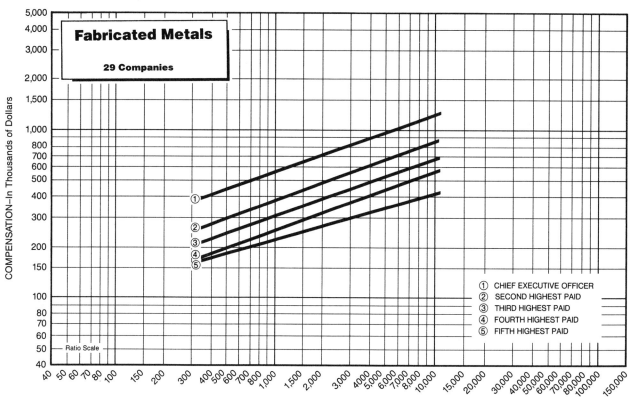

SALES–In Millions of Dollars

Table 58: 1988 Sales Volume

	Companies	
1988 Sales	Number	Percent
$5 billion and over	1	3%
2-4,999 billion	2	7
1-1,999 billion	6	21
500-999 million	4	14
300-499 million	6	21
200-299 million	7	24
199 million and under	3	10
Total	29	100%

	Middle 50% Range	
Median	Low	High
$414 million	$272 million	$1.1 billion

Table 59: 1988 Total Current Compensation

		Middle 50% Range	
Compensation Rank	Median	Low	High
CEO	$467,000	$327,000	$678,000
Second highest	295,000	241,000	450,000
Third highest	238,000	193,000	320,000
Fourth highest	197,000	164,000	244,000
Fifth highest	173,000	155,000	235,000

Table 60: 1988 Total Current Compensation Regression Formula

Compensation Rank	Formula	r^2
CEO	$\log Y = 1.7340 + 0.3410 \log X$	55%
Second highest	$\log Y = 1.5440 + 0.3450 \log X$	59
Third highest	$\log Y = 1.4730 + 0.3400 \log X$	53
Fourth highest	$\log Y = 1.3880 + 0.3400 \log X$	53
Fifth highest	$\log Y = 1.5110 + 0.2800 \log X$	43

Table 61: Total Current Compensation as a Percentage of CEO's Total Current Compensation

Compensation Rank	Median	Middle 50% Range	
		Low	High
Second highest	68%	54%	77%
Third highest	56	45	63
Fourth highest	43	36	54
Fifth highest	42	32	50

Table 62: 1988 Salary

Compensation Rank	Median	Middle 50% Range	
		Low	High
CEO	$300,000	$260,000	$460,000
Second highest	212,000	158,000	260,000
Third highest	178,000	152,000	205,000
Fourth highest	160,000	118,000	180,000
Fifth highest	135,000	110,000	170,000

Table 63: 1988 Salary Regression Formula

Compensation Rank	Formula	r^2
CEO	$\log Y = 1.7810 + 0.2630 \log X$	47%
Second highest	$\log Y = 1.6220 + 0.2510 \log X$	39
Third highest	$\log Y = 1.6290 + 0.2220 \log X$	45
Fourth highest	$\log Y = 1.6200 + 0.2040 \log X$	46
Fifth highest	$\log Y = 1.6730 + 0.1670 \log X$	30

Table 64: Salary as a Percentage of CEO's Salary

Compensation Rank	Median	Middle 50% Range	
		Low	High
Second highest	61%	53%	76%
Third highest	54	48	61
Fourth highest	47	43	57
Fifth highest	43	38	52

Food and Kindred Products

Chart 7: Total Current Compensation of the Five Highest-Paid Executives, by Company Sales

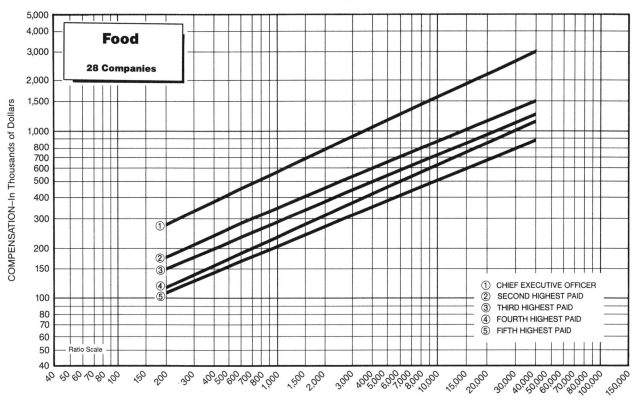

Food

28 Companies

COMPENSATION–In Thousands of Dollars

① CHIEF EXECUTIVE OFFICER
② SECOND HIGHEST PAID
③ THIRD HIGHEST PAID
④ FOURTH HIGHEST PAID
⑤ FIFTH HIGHEST PAID

Ratio Scale

SALES–In Millions of Dollars

Table 65: 1988 Sales Volume

1988 Sales	Companies Number	Companies Percent
$5 billion and over	11	39%
2-4,999 billion	5	18
1-1,999 billion	4	14
500-999 million	4	14
300-499 million	—	—
200-299 million	—	—
199 million and under	4	14
Total	28	100%

Median	Middle 50% Range Low	Middle 50% Range High
$2.2 billion	$738 million	$6.3 billion

Table 66: 1988 Total Current Compensation

Compensation Rank	Median	Middle 50% Range Low	Middle 50% Range High
CEO	$749,000	$609,000	$1,312,000
Second highest	502,000	291,000	805,000
Third highest	369,000	235,000	620,000
Fourth highest	342,000	193,000	544,000
Fifth highest	321,000	208,000	476,000

Table 67: 1988 Total Current Compensation Regression Formula

Compensation Rank	Formula	r^2
CEO	$\log Y = 1.4620 + 0.4330 \log X$	80%
Second highest	$\log Y = 1.2720 + 0.4210 \log X$	74
Third highest	$\log Y = 1.2560 + 0.4000 \log X$	76
Fourth highest	$\log Y = 1.1080 + 0.4200 \log X$	80
Fifth highest	$\log Y = 1.1270 + 0.3980 \log X$	76

Table 68: Total Current Compensation as a Percentage of CEO's Total Current Compensation

Compensation Rank	Median	Middle 50% Range	
		Low	High
Second highest	62%	44%	70%
Third highest	48	38	57
Fourth highest	40	34	47
Fifth highest	37	29	41

Table 69: 1988 Salary

Compensation Rank	Median	Middle 50% Range	
		Low	High
CEO	$467,000	$320,000	$650,000
Second highest	306,000	213,000	449,000
Third highest	250,000	180,000	363,000
Fourth highest	199,000	146,000	310,000
Fifth highest	198,000	146,000	273,000

Table 70: 1988 Salary Regression Formula

Compensation Rank	Formula	r^2
CEO	$\log Y = 1.8320 + 0.2520 \log X$	64%
Second highest	$\log Y = 1.4060 + 0.3210 \log X$	71
Third highest	$\log Y = 1.3240 + 0.3260 \log X$	74
Fourth highest	$\log Y = 1.3210 + 0.3000 \log X$	71
Fifth highest	$\log Y = 1.3590 + 0.2790 \log X$	73

Table 71: Salary as a Percentage of CEO's Salary

Compensation Rank	Median	Middle 50% Range	
		Low	High
Second highest	67%	62%	77%
Third highest	55	48	64
Fourth highest	46	40	53
Fifth highest	42	37	47

Industrial Chemicals

Chart 8: Total Current Compensation of the Five Highest-Paid Executives, by Company Sales

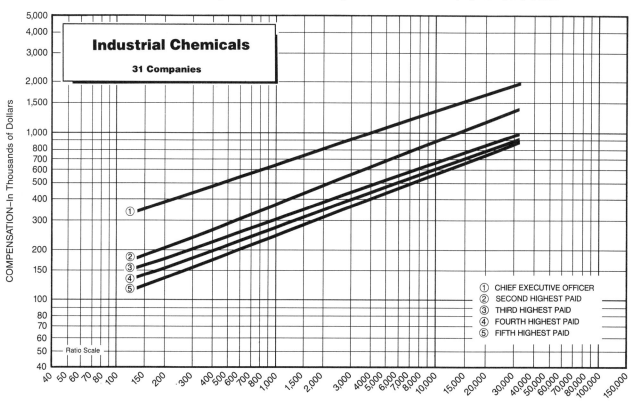

Industrial Chemicals

31 Companies

COMPENSATION–In Thousands of Dollars

Ratio Scale

SALES–In Millions of Dollars

① CHIEF EXECUTIVE OFFICER
② SECOND HIGHEST PAID
③ THIRD HIGHEST PAID
④ FOURTH HIGHEST PAID
⑤ FIFTH HIGHEST PAID

Table 72: 1988 Sales Volume

1988 Sales	Companies	
	Number	Percent
$5 billion and over	3	10%
2-4,999 billion	6	19
1-1,999 billion	7	23
500-999 million	5	16
300-499 million	6	19
200-299 million	3	10
199 million and under	1	3
Total	31	100%

Median	Middle 50% Range	
	Low	High
$1.0 billion	$383 million	$1.7 billion

Table 73: 1988 Total Current Compensation

Compensation Rank	Median	Middle 50% Range	
		Low	High
CEO	$664,000	$503,000	$875,000
Second highest	389,000	253,000	575,000
Third highest	291,000	210,000	443,000
Fourth highest	261,000	192,000	409,000
Fifth highest	250,000	173,000	357,000

Table 74: 1988 Total Current Compensation Regression Formula

Compensation Rank	Formula	r^2
CEO	$\log Y = 1.8700 + 0.3130 \log X$	72%
Second highest	$\log Y = 1.4620 + 0.3730 \log X$	80
Third highest	$\log Y = 1.5010 + 0.3280 \log X$	73
Fourth highest	$\log Y = 1.4060 + 0.3410 \log X$	80
Fifth highest	$\log Y = 1.2890 + 0.3650 \log X$	82

Table 75: Total Current Compensation as a Percentage of CEO's Total Current Compensation

Compensation Rank	Median	Middle 50% Range	
		Low	High
Second highest	61%	53%	69%
Third highest	50	44	56
Fourth highest	44	37	49
Fifth highest	37	33	45

Table 76: 1988 Salary

Compensation Rank	Median	Middle 50% Range	
		Low	High
CEO	$375,000	$340,000	$475,000
Second highest	250,000	163,000	314,000
Third highest	187,000	147,000	253,000
Fourth highest	175,000	127,000	234,000
Fifth highest	169,000	131,000	221,000

Table 77: 1988 Salary Regression Formula

Compensation Rank	Formula	r^2
CEO	$\log Y = 1.8220 + 0.2590 \log X$	71%
Second highest	$\log Y = 1.4500 + 0.3120 \log X$	77
Third highest	$\log Y = 1.4680 + 0.2770 \log X$	69
Fourth highest	$\log Y = 1.3750 + 0.2980 \log X$	75
Fifth highest	$\log Y = 1.3840 + 0.2860 \log X$	73

Table 78: Salary as a Percentage of CEO's Salary

Compensation Rank	Median	Middle 50% Range	
		Low	High
Second highest	63%	59%	67%
Third highest	52	44	57
Fourth highest	46	44	52
Fifth highest	44	42	48

Machinery (except Electrical)

Chart 9: Total Current Compensation of the Five Highest-Paid Executives, by Company Sales

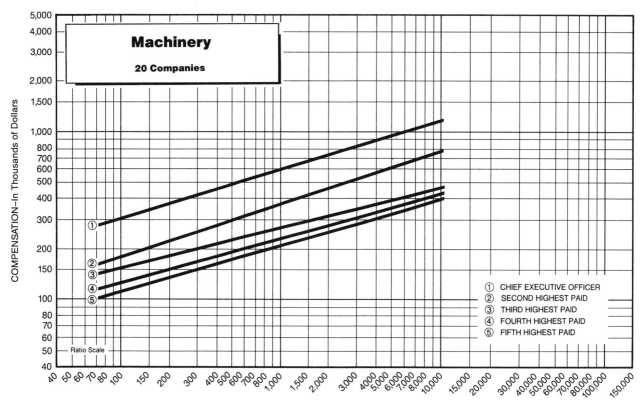

SALES–In Millions of Dollars

Table 79: 1988 Sales Volume

1988 Sales	Companies Number	Companies Percent
$5 billion and over	2	10%
2-4,999 billion	6	30
1-1,999 billion	—	—
500-999 million	4	20
300-499 million	1	5
200-299 million	2	10
199 million and under	5	25
Total	20	100%

Median	Middle 50% Range Low	Middle 50% Range High
$520 million	$195 million	$3.3 billion

Table 80: 1988 Total Current Compensation

Compensation Rank	Median	Middle 50% Range Low	Middle 50% Range High
CEO	$450,000	$319,000	$875,000
Second highest	300,000	218,000	585,000
Third highest	227,000	176,000	353,000
Fourth highest	200,000	145,000	326,000
Fifth highest	190,000	131,000	297,000

Table 81: 1988 Total Current Compensation Regression Formula

Compensation Rank	Formula	r^2
CEO	log Y = 1.9200 + 0.2840 log X	40%
Second highest	log Y = 1.6090 + 0.3190 log X	64
Third highest	log Y = 1.6940 + 0.2440 log X	65
Fourth highest	log Y = 1.5540 + 0.2700 log X	72
Fifth highest	log Y = 1.4940 + 0.2750 log X	82

Table 82: Total Current Compensation as a Percentage of CEO's Total Current Compensation

Compensation Rank	Median	Middle 50% Range	
		Low	High
Second highest	62%	51%	81%
Third highest	49	44	57
Fourth highest	43	39	48
Fifth highest	35	32	44

Table 83: 1988 Salary

Compensation Rank	Median	Middle 50% Range	
		Low	High
CEO	$425,000	$283,000	$567,000
Second highest		Insufficient data	
Third highest	227,000	150,000	250,000
Fourth highest		Insufficient data	
Fifth highest		Insufficient data	

Table 84: 1988 Salary Regression Formula

Compensation Rank	Formula	r^2
CEO	log Y = 2.1460 + 0.1580 log X	48%
Second highest	log Y = 1.7190 + 0.2460 log X	49
Third highest	log Y = 1.8520 + 0.1590 log X	49
Fourth highest	log Y = 1.7080 + 0.1910 log X	72
Fifth highest	log Y = 1.6690 + 0.1930 log X	71

Table 85: Salary as a Percentage of CEO's Salary

Compensation Rank	Median	Middle 50% Range	
		Low	High
Second highest	72%	59%	79%
Third highest	57	49	58
Fourth highest	50	42	52
Fifth highest	50	34	51

Paper

Chart 10: Total Current Compensation of the Five Highest-Paid Executives, by Company Sales

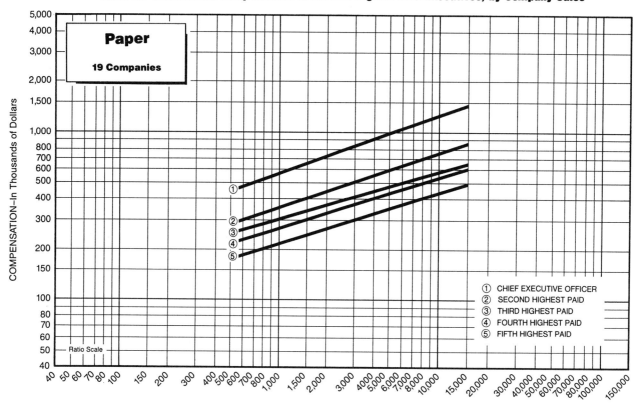

SALES–In Millions of Dollars

Table 86: 1988 Sales Volume

1988 Sales	Companies	
	Number	Percent
$5 billion and over	6	32%
2-4,999 billion	4	21
1-1,999 billion	4	21
500-999 million	5	26
Total	19	100%

	Middle 50% Range	
Median	Low	High
$2.7 billion	$897 million	$5.1 billion

Table 87: 1988 Total Current Compensation

Compensation Rank	Median	Middle 50% Range	
		Low	High
CEO	$792,000	$484,000	$1,128,000
Second highest	493,000	366,000	670,000
Third highest	422,000	327,000	495,000
Fourth highest	414,000	260,000	450,000
Fifth highest	310,000	218,000	403,000

Table 88: 1988 Total Current Compensation Regression Formula

Compensation Rank	Formula	r^2
CEO	log Y = 1.7150 + 0.3470 log X	53%
Second highest	log Y = 1.5920 + 0.3200 log X	52
Third highest	log Y = 1.6570 + 0.2740 log X	45
Fourth highest	log Y = 1.5310 + 0.2960 log X	49
Fifth highest	log Y = 1.4280 + 0.3020 log X	47

Table 89: Total Current Compensation as a Percentage of CEO's Total Current Compensation

Compensation Rank	Median	Middle 50% Range	
		Low	High
Second highest	60%	54%	70%
Third highest	50	41	54
Fourth highest	42	37	47
Fifth highest	36	33	41

Table 90: 1988 Salary

Compensation Rank	Median	Middle 50% Range	
		Low	High
CEO	$478,000	$390,000	$650,000
Second highest	286,000	240,000	360,000
Third highest	245,000	179,000	318,000
Fourth highest	228,000	162,000	260,000
Fifth highest	210,000	156,000	230,000

Table 91: 1988 Salary Regression Formula

Compensation Rank	Formula	r^2
CEO	log Y = 1.6680 + 0.3030 log X	71%
Second highest	log Y = 1.4630 + 0.2980 log X	71
Third highest	log Y = 1.4870 + 0.2650 log X	64
Fourth highest	log Y = 1.4560 + 0.2610 log X	66
Fifth highest	log Y = 1.6720 + 0.1740 log X	16

Table 92: Salary as a Percentage of CEO's Salary

Compensation Rank	Median	Middle 50% Range	
		Low	High
Second highest	57%	51%	74%
Third highest	50	42	57
Fourth highest	42	39	45
Fifth highest	37	34	41

Plastic, Rubber, and Leather Products

Chart 11: Total Current Compensation of the Five Highest-Paid Executives, by Company Sales

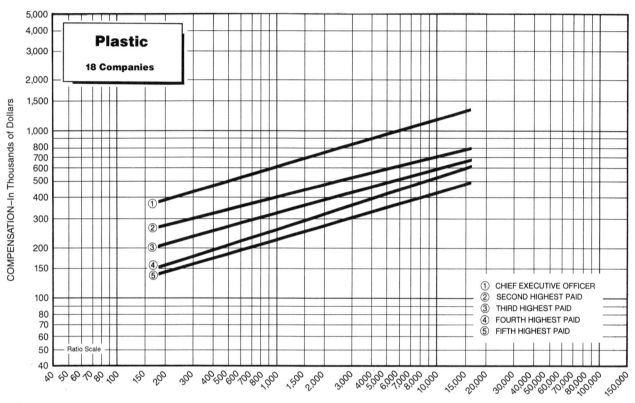

Plastic

18 Companies

① CHIEF EXECUTIVE OFFICER
② SECOND HIGHEST PAID
③ THIRD HIGHEST PAID
④ FOURTH HIGHEST PAID
⑤ FIFTH HIGHEST PAID

COMPENSATION–In Thousands of Dollars

SALES–In Millions of Dollars

Ratio Scale

Table 93: 1988 Sales Volume

1988 Sales	Companies Number	Companies Percent
$5 billion and over	2	11%
2-4,999 billion	2	11
1-1,999 billion	5	28
500-999 million	3	17
300-499 million	2	11
200-299 million	3	17
199 million and under	1	6
Total	18	100%

Median	Middle 50% Range Low	Middle 50% Range High
$748 million	$388 million	$1.9 billion

Table 94: 1988 Total Current Compensation

Compensation Rank	Median	Middle 50% Range Low	Middle 50% Range High
CEO	$598,000	$377,000	$985,000
Second highest	431,000	348,000	489,000
Third highest	341,000	220,000	424,000
Fourth highest	272,000	175,000	345,000
Fifth highest	229,000	164,000	305,000

Table 95: 1988 Total Current Compensation Regression Formula

Compensation Rank	Formula	r^2
CEO	$\log Y = 1.9110 + 0.2930 \log X$	43%
Second highest	$\log Y = 1.9020 + 0.2360 \log X$	50
Third highest	$\log Y = 1.7020 + 0.2680 \log X$	64
Fourth highest	$\log Y = 1.4480 + 0.3220 \log X$	73
Fifth highest	$\log Y = 1.4950 + 0.2860 \log X$	65

Table 96: Total Current Compensation as a Percentage of CEO's Total Current Compensation

Compensation Rank	Median	Middle 50% Range	
		Low	High
Second highest	67%	58%	87%
Third highest	51	45	64
Fourth highest	44	36	53
Fifth highest	35	33	47

Table 97: 1988 Salary

Compensation Rank	Median	Middle 50% Range	
		Low	High
CEO	$370,000	$246,000	$583,000
Second highest	264,000	190,000	315,000
Third highest	200,000	165,000	279,000
Fourth highest	150,000	128,000	237,000
Fifth highest	129,000	100,000	217,000

Table 98: 1988 Salary Regression Formula

Compensation Rank	Formula	r^2
CEO	$\log Y = 1.9180 + 0.2260 \log X$	25%
Second highest	$\log Y = 1.8110 + 0.2020 \log X$	50
Third highest	$\log Y = 1.5520 + 0.2500 \log X$	59
Fourth highest	$\log Y = 1.3590 + 0.2860 \log X$	70
Fifth highest	$\log Y = 1.4750 + 0.2330 \log X$	58

Table 99: Salary as a Percentage of CEO's Salary

Compensation Rank	Median	Middle 50% Range	
		Low	High
Second highest	73%	59%	81%
Third highest	56	48	61
Fourth highest	47	39	50
Fifth highest	41	35	47

Primary Metals (including Steel)

Chart 12: Total Current Compensation of the Five Highest-Paid Executives, by Company Sales

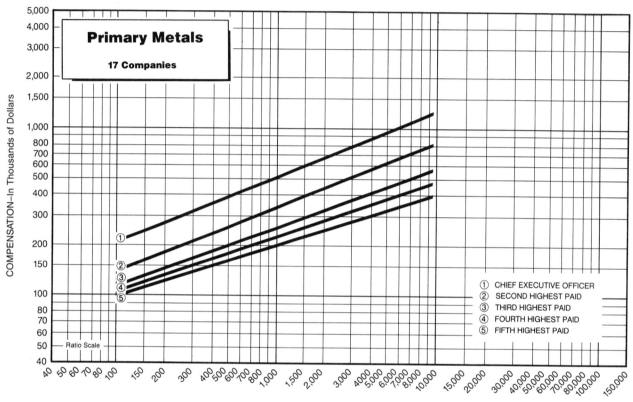

SALES—In Millions of Dollars

Table 100: 1988 Sales Volume

1988 Sales	Companies	
	Number	Percent
$5 billion and over	4	24%
2-4,999 billion	3	18
1-1,999 billion	4	24
500-999 million..........................	1	6
300-499 million..........................	3	18
200-299 million..........................	1	6
199 million and under	1	6
Total	17	100%

Median	Middle 50% Range	
	Low	High
$1.2 billion	$495 million	$4.1 billion

Table 101: 1988 Total Current Compensation

Compensation Rank	Median	Middle 50% Range	
		Low	High
CEO	$678,000	$376,000	$940,000
Second highest	502,000	224,000	552,000
Third highest	387,000	224,000	459,000
Fourth highest	270,000	185,000	417,000
Fifth highest	241,000	153,000	365,000

Table 102: 1988 Total Current Compensation Regression Formula

Compensation Rank	Formula	r^2
CEO	$\log Y = 1.5380 + 0.3910 \log X$	61%
Second highest	$\log Y = 1.3880 + 0.3800 \log X$	60
Third highest	$\log Y = 1.3410 + 0.3570 \log X$	67
Fourth highest	$\log Y = 1.3890 + 0.3220 \log X$	65
Fifth highest	$\log Y = 1.3950 + 0.3050 \log X$	59

Table 103: Total Current Compensation as a Percentage of CEO's Total Current Compensation

Compensation Rank	Median	Middle 50% Range	
		Low	High
Second highest	67%	55%	75%
Third highest	51	40	59
Fourth highest	40	34	49
Fifth highest	37	30	42

Table 104: 1988 Salary

Compensation Rank	Median	Middle 50% Range	
		Low	High
CEO	$456,000	$266,000	$505,000
Second highest	260,000	160,000	335,000
Third highest	200,000	145,000	264,000
Fourth highest	185,000	130,000	225,000
Fifth highest	185,000	100,000	222,000

Table 105: 1988 Salary Regression Formula

Compensation Rank	Formula	r^2
CEO	$\log Y = 1.7340 + 0.2790 \log X$	54%
Second highest	$\log Y = 1.5820 + 0.2640 \log X$	42
Third highest	$\log Y = 1.5010 + 0.2550 \log X$	50
Fourth highest	$\log Y = 1.4530 + 0.2560 \log X$	65
Fifth highest	$\log Y = 1.2400 + 0.3130 \log X$	69

Table 106: Salary as a Percentage of CEO's Salary

Compensation Rank	Median	Middle 50% Range	
		Low	High
Second highest	67%	57%	75%
Third highest	53	50	57
Fourth highest	49	43	52
Fifth highest	45	43	49

Transportation Equipment

Chart 13: Total Current Compensation of the Five Highest-Paid Executives, by Company Sales

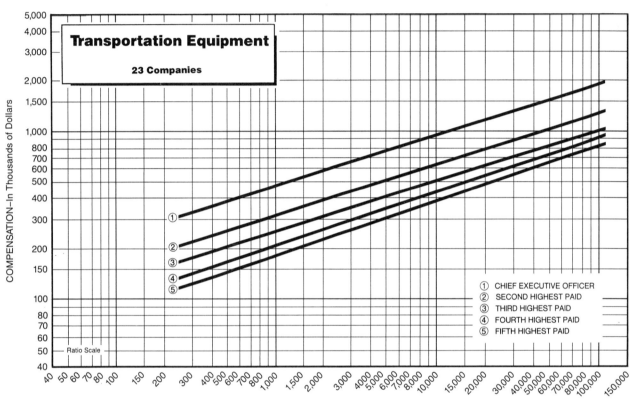

SALES–In Millions of Dollars

Table 107: 1988 Sales Volume

	Companies	
1988 Sales	Number	Percent
$5 billion and over	5	22%
2-4,999 billion	6	26
1-1,999 billion	4	17
500-999 million	3	13
300-499 million	4	17
200-299 million	1	4
Total	23	100%

	Middle 50% Range	
Median	Low	High
$1.4 billion	$715 million	$4.1 billion

Table 108: 1988 Total Current Compensation

		Middle 50% Range	
Compensation Rank	Median	Low	High
CEO	$613,000	$415,000	$1,002,000
Second highest	362,000	240,000	633,000
Third highest	326,000	192,000	490,000
Fourth highest	311,000	178,000	424,000
Fifth highest	260,000	132,000	388,000

Table 109: 1988 Total Current Compensation Regression Formula

Compensation Rank	Formula	r^2
CEO	$\log Y = 1.7570 + 0.3090 \log X$	63%
Second highest	$\log Y = 1.6060 + 0.2980 \log X$	63
Third highest	$\log Y = 1.4870 + 0.3040 \log X$	73
Fourth highest	$\log Y = 1.3680 + 0.3200 \log X$	74
Fifth highest	$\log Y = 1.2860 + 0.3260 \log X$	68

Table 110: Total Current Compensation as a Percentage of CEO's Total Current Compensation

Compensation Rank	Median	Middle 50% Range	
		Low	High
Second highest	71%	58%	79%
Third highest	55	41	67
Fourth highest	48	35	57
Fifth highest	39	31	52

Table 111: 1988 Salary

Compensation Rank	Median	Middle 50% Range	
		Low	High
CEO	$425,000	$385,000	$900,000
Second highest	295,000	200,000	580,000
Third highest	186,000	151,000	417,000
Fourth highest	220,000	120,000	291,000
Fifth highest	175,000	110,000	278,000

Table 112: 1988 Salary Regression Formula

Compensation Rank	Formula	r^2
CEO	$\log Y = 1.6600 + 0.2870 \log X$	68%
Second highest	$\log Y = 1.4340 + 0.2910 \log X$	72
Third highest	$\log Y = 1.2930 + 0.2860 \log X$	60
Fourth highest	$\log Y = 1.1910 + 0.3080 \log X$	84
Fifth highest	$\log Y = 1.1210 + 0.3170 \log X$	71

Table 113: Salary as a Percentage of CEO's Salary

Compensation Rank	Median	Middle 50% Range	
		Low	High
Second highest	67%	37%	79%
Third highest	41	27	48
Fourth highest	38	27	52
Fifth highest	34	27	42

Chapter 6
Commercial Banking

Chart 14: Total Current Compensation of the Five Highest-Paid Executives, by Total Assets

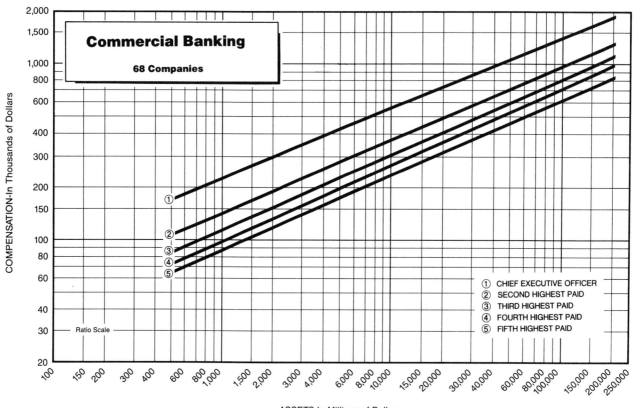

ASSETS-In Millions of Dollars

Table 114: 1988 Total Assets

1988 Total Assets	Companies	
	Number	Percent
$5 billion and over	36	53%
2-4,999 billion	18	26
1-1,999 billion	8	12
500-999 million	6	9
Total	68	100%

Median	Middle 50% Range	
	Low	High
$5.2 billion	$2.2 billion	$10.7 billion

Table 115: 1988 Total Current Compensation

Compensation Rank	Median	Middle 50% Range	
		Low	High
CEO	$482,000	$283,000	$676,000
Second highest	267,000	181,000	444,000
Third highest	228,000	157,000	349,000
Fourth highest	198,000	124,000	309,000
Fifth highest	172,000	114,000	262,000

Table 116: 1988 Total Current Compensation Regression Formula

Compensation Rank	Formula	r^2
CEO	$\log Y = 1.1540 + 0.4020 \log X$	73%
Second highest	$\log Y = 0.8890 + 0.4220 \log X$	76
Third highest	$\log Y = 0.7670 + 0.4330 \log X$	81
Fourth highest	$\log Y = 0.6930 + 0.4350 \log X$	83
Fifth highest	$\log Y = 0.6500 + 0.4300 \log X$	85

Table 117: Total Current Compensation as a Percentage of CEO's Total Current Compensation

Compensation Rank	Median	Middle 50% Range Low	Middle 50% Range High
Second highest	65%	55%	74%
Third highest	54	45	62
Fourth highest	46	39	53
Fifth highest	40	33	48

Table 118: 1988 Salary

Compensation Rank	Median	Middle 50% Range Low	Middle 50% Range High
CEO	$340,000	$238,000	$436,000
Second highest	250,000	149,000	309,000
Third highest	195,000	122,000	250,000
Fourth highest	150,000	113,000	229,000
Fifth highest	140,000	104,000	198,000

Table 119: 1988 Salary Regression Formula

Compensation Rank	Formula	r^2
CEO	$\log Y = 1.3680 + 0.3090 \log X$	77%
Second highest	$\log Y = 1.1040 + 0.3350 \log X$	75
Third highest	$\log Y = 0.9610 + 0.3490 \log X$	83
Fourth highest	$\log Y = 0.9340 + 0.3430 \log X$	83
Fifth highest	$\log Y = 0.8620 + 0.3490 \log X$	82

Table 120: Salary as a Percentage of CEO's Salary

Compensation Rank	Median	Middle 50% Range Low	Middle 50% Range High
Second highest	68%	57%	74%
Third highest	56	48	66
Fourth highest	48	41	55
Fifth highest	42	36	50

Table 121: 1988 Bonus Awards (as Percent of Salary), by Company Size

Executive	Total Assets — Low $2.2 Billion	Total Assets — Median $5.2 Billion	Total Assets — High $10.7 Billion
CEO			
1988 Bonus	34%	43%	50%
Salary	$258,000	$332,000	$412,000
Second Highest			
1988 Bonus	27%	35%	43%
Salary	$170,000	$224,000	$282,000
Third Highest			
1988 Bonus	28%	36%	43%
Salary	$137,000	$183,000	$234,000
Fourth Highest			
1988 Bonus	22%	30%	38%
Salary	$122,000	$162,000	$207,000
Fifth Highest			
1988 Bonus	19%	27%	33%
Salary	$108,000	$145,000	$185,000

Table 122: 1988 Bonus Awards

1988 Bonus Awards (Percent of Salary)	CEOS		Second Highest Paid		Third Highest Paid		Fourth Highest Paid		Fifth Highest Paid	
	Number	Percent	Number	Percent	Number	Percent	Number	Percent	Number	Percent
100% or more	4	8%	1	2%	1	2%	–	–	–	–
70-99	4	8	4	8	7	13	4	8%	4	8%
60-69	7	14	2	4	1	2	2	4	1	2
50-59	8	16	7	14	4	8	3	6	3	6
40-49	11	22	13	25	14	26	10	19	7	14
30-39	6	12	11	22	10	19	13	25	10	20
20-29	8	16	6	12	8	15	9	17	8	16
Less than 20%	3	6	7	14	8	15	11	21	17	34
Total	51	100%	51	100%	53	100%	52	100%	50	100%
Median Bonus	47%		40%		40%		32%		28%	
Middle 50% Range	33 – 60%		28 – 52%		27 – 49%		22 – 46%		17 – 40%	

Chapter 7
Communications

Chart 15: Total Current Compensation of the Five Highest-Paid Executives, by Company Sales

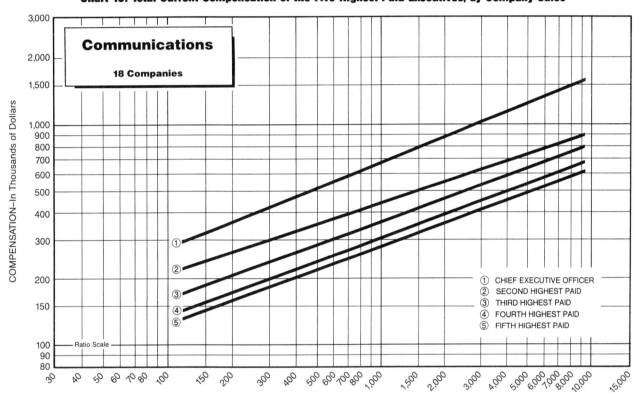

SALES–In Millions of Dollars

Table 123: 1988 Sales Volume

1988 Sales	Companies	
	Number	Percent
$2 billion and over	3	17%
1-1,999 billion	3	17
500-999 million	1	6
300-499 million	7	39
200-299 million	1	6
199 million and under	3	17
Total	18	100%

Median	Middle 50% Range	
	Low	High
$402 million	$320 million	$1.8 billion

Table 124: 1988 Total Current Compensation

Compensation Rank	Median	Middle 50% Range	
		Low	High
CEO	$426,000	$365,000	$1,034,000
Second highest	318,000	250,000	591,000
Third highest	250,000	210,000	465,000
Fourth highest	240,000	160,000	429,000
Fifth highest	210,000	160,000	308,000

Table 125: 1988 Total Compensation Regression Formula

Compensation Rank	Formula	r^2
CEO	$\log Y = 1.6700 + 0.3870 \log X$	61%
Second highest	$\log Y = 1.6740 + 0.3230 \log X$	50
Third highest	$\log Y = 1.4990 + 0.3520 \log X$	59
Fourth highest	$\log Y = 1.4290 + 0.3530 \log X$	53
Fifth highest	$\log Y = 1.3790 + 0.3540 \log X$	59

Table 126: Total Current Compensation as a Percentage of CEO's Total Current Compensation

Compensation Rank	Median	Middle 50% Range	
		Low	High
Second highest	69%	56%	78%
Third highest	57	43	67
Fourth highest	43	40	56
Fifth highest	41	37	44

Table 127: 1988 Salary

Compensation Rank	Median	Middle 50% Range	
		Low	High
CEO	$375,000	$350,000	$630,000
Second highest	250,000	232,000	365,000
Third highest	250,000	218,000	330,000
Fourth highest	260,000	151,000	315,000
Fifth highest	210,000	150,000	320,000

Table 128: 1988 Salary Regression Formula

Compensation Rank	Formula	r^2
CEO	$\log Y = 1.8950 + 0.2620 \log X$	73%
Second highest	$\log Y = 1.9180 + 0.1870 \log X$	43
Third highest	$\log Y = 1.7590 + 0.2340 \log X$	35
Fourth highest	$\log Y = 1.7980 + 0.1890 \log X$	35
Fifth highest	$\log Y = 1.6540 + 0.2230 \log X$	42

Table 129: Salary as a Percentage of CEO's Salary

Compensation Rank	Median	Middle 50% Range	
		Low	High
Second highest	46%	45%	70%
Third highest	46	41	48
Fourth highest	45	44	47
Fifth highest	40	36	44

Chapter 8
Diversified Service

Chart 16: Total Current Compensation of the Five Highest-Paid Executives, by Company Sales

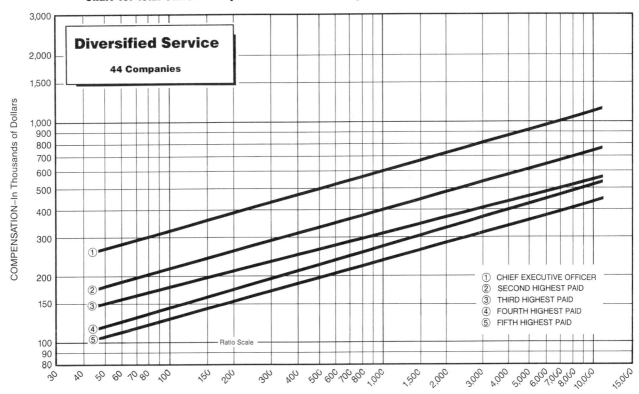

SALES–In Millions of Dollars

Table 130: 1988 Sales Volume

1988 Sales	Companies	
	Number	Percent
$5 billion and over	5	11%
2-4,999 billion	6	14
1-1,999 billion.........................	4	9
500-999 million	11	25
300-499 million	7	16
200-299 million	3	7
199 million and under	8	18
Total	44	100%

	Middle 50% Range	
Median	Low	High
$636 million	$272 million	$1.6 billion

Table 131: 1988 Total Current Compensation

Compensation Rank	Median	Middle 50% Range	
		Low	High
CEO	$479,000	$373,000	$863,000
Second highest	380,000	257,000	550,000
Third highest	273,000	198,000	384,000
Fourth highest	241,000	173,000	340,000
Fifth highest	207,000	154,000	295,000

Table 132: 1988 Total Current Compensation Regression Formula

Compensation Rank	Formula	r^2
CEO	$\log Y = 1.9680 + 0.2680 \log X$	49%
Second highest	$\log Y = 1.8190 + 0.2620 \log X$	46
Third highest	$\log Y = 1.7530 + 0.2460 \log X$	47
Fourth highest	$\log Y = 1.5800 + 0.2840 \log X$	59
Fifth highest	$\log Y = 1.5620 + 0.2690 \log X$	52

Table 133: Total Current Compensation as a Percentage of CEO's Total Current Compensation

Compensation Rank	Median	Middle 50% Range Low	Middle 50% Range High
Second highest	69%	56%	80%
Third highest	53	42	66
Fourth highest	46	38	54
Fifth highest	39	32	48

Table 134: 1988 Salary

Compensation Rank	Median	Middle 50% Range Low	Middle 50% Range High
CEO	$358,000	$241,000	$559,000
Second highest	251,000	175,000	344,000
Third highest	185,000	150,000	250,000
Fourth highest	175,000	140,000	240,000
Fifth highest	162,000	112,000	225,000

Table 135: 1988 Salary Regression Formula

Compensation Rank	Formula	r^2
CEO	$\log Y = 1.9020 + 0.2280 \log X$	48%
Second highest	$\log Y = 1.7750 + 0.2150 \log X$	46
Third highest	$\log Y = 1.7590 + 0.1910 \log X$	51
Fourth highest	$\log Y = 1.6040 + 0.2220 \log X$	60
Fifth highest	$\log Y = 1.5950 + 0.2110 \log X$	49

Table 136: Salary as a Percentage of CEO's Salary

Compensation Rank	Median	Middle 50% Range Low	Middle 50% Range High
Second highest	74%	56%	83%
Third highest	56	48	71
Fourth highest	49	41	60
Fifth highest	45	39	57

Table 137: 1988 Bonus Awards (as Percent of Salary), by Company Size

Executive	Sales Volume Middle 50% Range Low $272 Million	Sales Volume Middle 50% Range Median $636 Million	Sales Volume Middle 50% Range High $1.6 Billion
CEO			
1988 Bonus	51%	54%	56%
Salary	$287,000	$351,000	$437,000
Second Highest			
1988 Bonus	49%	52%	55%
Salary	$199,000	$239,000	$291,000
Third Highest			
1988 Bonus	38%	43%	47%
Salary	$169,000	$199,000	$236,000
Fourth Highest			
1988 Bonus	38%	43%	48%
Salary	$145,000	$173,000	$208,000
Fifth Highest			
1988 Bonus	31%	37%	43%
Salary	$136,000	$159,000	$188,000

Table 138: 1988 Bonus Awards

1988 Bonus Awards (Percent of Salary)	CEOS		Second Highest Paid		Third Highest Paid		Fourth Highest Paid		Fifth Highest Paid	
	Number	Percent	Number	Percent	Number	Percent	Number	Percent	Number	Percent
100% or more	7	18%	8	21%	2	5%	2	5%	3	9%
70-99	8	21	7	18	8	22	5	13	5	14
40-69	10	26	8	21	12	32	13	33	10	29
20-39	9	24	10	26	11	30	13	33	11	31
Less than 20%	4	11	5	13	4	11	6	15	6	17
Total	38	100%	38	100%	37	100%	39	100%	35	100%
Median Bonus	50%		50%		42%		40%		40%	
Middle 50% Range	36 – 89%		29 – 83%		29 – 70%		25 – 62%		28 – 69%	

Chapter 9

Energy and Natural Resources

Chart 17: Total Current Compensation of the Five Highest-Paid Executives, by Company Sales

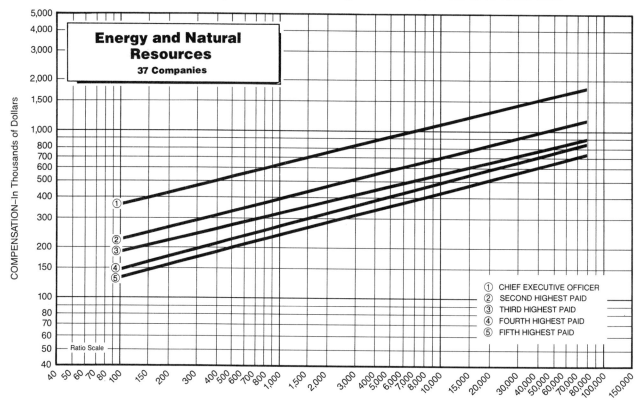

SALES–In Millions of Dollars

Table 139: 1988 Sales Volume

1988 Sales	Companies	
	Number	Percent
$5 billion and over	14	38%
2-4,999 billion	5	14
1-1,999 billion	9	24
500-999 million	2	5
300-499 million	1	3
200-299 million	—	—
199 million and under	6	16
Total	37	100%

Median	Middle 50% Range	
	Low	High
$2.1 billion	$1.2 billion	$11.3 billion

Table 140: 1988 Total Current Compensation

Compensation Rank	Median	Middle 50% Range	
		Low	High
CEO	$796,000	$570,000	$1,175,000
Second highest	572,000	289,000	804,000
Third highest	442,000	259,000	580,000
Fourth highest	341,000	212,000	511,000
Fifth highest	298,000	210,000	471,000

Table 141: 1988 Total Current Compensation Regression Formula

Compensation Rank	Formula	r^2
CEO	$\log Y = 2.0860 + 0.2380 \log X$	57%
Second highest	$\log Y = 1.8180 + 0.2590 \log X$	47
Third highest	$\log Y = 1.6850 + 0.2640 \log X$	53
Fourth highest	$\log Y = 1.6340 + 0.2640 \log X$	53
Fifth highest	$\log Y = 1.6030 + 0.2570 \log X$	58

Table 142: Total Current Compensation as a Percentage of CEO's Total Current Compensation

Compensation Rank	Median	Middle 50% Range	
		Low	High
Second highest	65%	51%	79%
Third highest	48	39	61
Fourth highest	45	34	50
Fifth highest	40	32	47

Table 143: 1988 Salary

Compensation Rank	Median	Middle 50% Range	
		Low	High
CEO	$552,000	$395,000	$775,000
Second highest	325,000	220,000	550,000
Third highest	288,000	190,000	450,000
Fourth highest	230,000	159,000	369,000
Fifth highest	210,000	150,000	345,000

Table 144: 1988 Salary Regression Formula

Compensation Rank	Formula	r^2
CEO	$\log Y = 2.0880 + 0.1860 \log X$	62%
Second highest	$\log Y = 1.6800 + 0.2480 \log X$	61
Third highest	$\log Y = 1.5940 + 0.2450 \log X$	62
Fourth highest	$\log Y = 1.5380 + 0.2440 \log X$	64
Fifth highest	$\log Y = 1.4910 + 0.2490 \log X$	71

Table 145: Salary as a Percentage of CEO's Salary

Compensation Rank	Median	Middle 50% Range	
		Low	High
Second highest	64%	56%	76%
Third highest	53	43	63
Fourth highest	50	36	55
Fifth highest	43	35	53

Table 146: 1988 Bonus Awards (as Percent of Salary), by Company Size

	Sales Volume		
	Middle 50% Range		
	Low	Median	High
	$1.2	$2.1	$11.3
Executive	Billion	Billion	Billion
CEO			
1988 Bonus	49%	45%	72%
Salary	$432,000	$484,000	$682,000
Second Highest			
1988 Bonus	45%	49%	65%
Salary	$265,000	$305,000	$466,000
Third Highest			
1988 Bonus	43%	48%	60%
Salary	$214,000	$247,000	$379,000
Fourth Highest			
1988 Bonus	43%	48%	65%
Salary	$183,000	$212,000	$331,000
Fifth Highest			
1988 Bonus	30%	35%	51%
Salary	$170,000	$198,000	$315,000

Table 147: 1988 Bonus Awards

1988 Bonus Awards (Percent of Salary)	CEOS		Second Highest Paid		Third Highest Paid		Fourth Highest Paid		Fifth Highest Paid	
	Number	Percent	Number	Percent	Number	Percent	Number	Percent	Number	Percent
100% or more	4	17%	2	8%	2	8%	1	4%	—	—
70-99	7	29	7	29	6	23	7	27	3	13%
40-69	8	33	11	46	10	38	8	31	11	48
20-39	3	13	2	8	3	12	6	23	5	22
Less than 20%	2	8	2	8	5	19	4	15	4	17
Total	24	100%	24	100%	26	100%	26	100%	23	100%
Median Bonus	64%		60%		53%		53%		49%	
Middle 50% Range	44 – 78%		42 – 75%		27 – 71%		30 – 74%		28 – 62%	

Chapter 10
Insurance

Chart 18: Total Current Compensation of the Five Highest-Paid Executives, by Premium Income

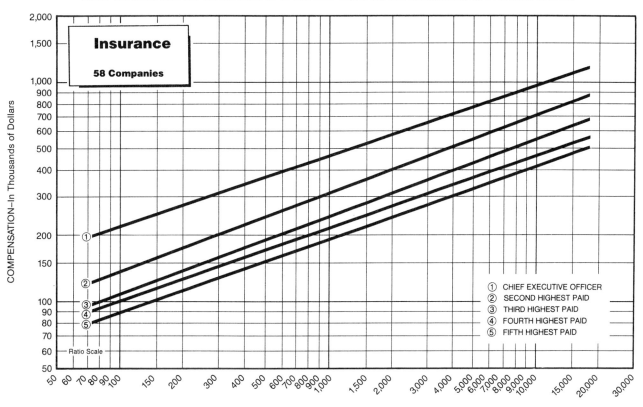

TOTAL PREMIUM INCOME–In Millions of Dollars

Table 148: 1988 Premium Income

	Companies	
1988 Premium Income	Number	Percent
$5 billion and over	7	12%
2-4,999 billion	6	10
1-1,999 billion	8	14
500-999 million	10	17
300-499 million	11	19
200-299 million	5	9
199 million and under	11	19
Total	58	100%

	Middle 50% Range	
Median	Low	High
$563 million	$255 million	$1.9 million

Table 149: 1988 Total Current Compensation

		Middle 50% Range	
Compensation Rank	Median	Low	High
CEO	$422,000	$285,000	$650,000
Second highest	262,000	162,000	465,000
Third highest	208,000	141,000	385,000
Fourth highest	186,000	113,000	294,000
Fifth highest	170,000	101,000	270,000

Table 150: 1988 Total Current Compensation Regression Formula

Compensation Rank	Formula	r^2
CEO	$\log Y = 1.6800 + 0.3290 \log X$	55%
Second highest	$\log Y = 1.4140 + 0.3600 \log X$	60
Third highest	$\log Y = 1.3270 + 0.3540 \log X$	63
Fourth highest	$\log Y = 1.3200 + 0.3350 \log X$	67
Fifth highest	$\log Y = 1.2800 + 0.3330 \log X$	69

Table 151: Total Current Compensation as a Percentage of CEO's Total Current Compensation

Compensation Rank	Median	Middle 50% Range Low	Middle 50% Range High
Second highest	66%	58%	76%
Third highest	50	46	62
Fourth highest	45	40	53
Fifth highest	41	35	47

Table 152: 1988 Salary

Compensation Rank	Median	Middle 50% Range Low	Middle 50% Range High
CEO	$320,000	$225,000	$540,000
Second highest	205,000	140,000	335,000
Third highest	154,000	115,000	285,000
Fourth highest	143,000	100,000	215,000
Fifth highest	125,000	95,000	217,000

Table 153: 1988 Salary Regression Formula

Compensation Rank	Formula	r^2
CEO	$\log Y = 1.6770 + 0.2940 \log X$	60%
Second highest	$\log Y = 1.4800 + 0.2990 \log X$	56
Third highest	$\log Y = 1.3760 + 0.3020 \log X$	64
Fourth highest	$\log Y = 1.3670 + 0.2850 \log X$	71
Fifth highest	$\log Y = 1.3210 + 0.2870 \log X$	68

Table 154: Salary as a Percentage of CEO's Salary

Compensation Rank	Median	Middle 50% Range Low	Middle 50% Range High
Second highest	64%	55%	73%
Third highest	52	48	59
Fourth highest	46	40	52
Fifth highest	42	35	48

Table 155: 1988 Bonus Awards (as Percent of Salary), by Company Size

Executive	Premium Income Low $255 Million	Premium Income Median $563 Million	Premium Income High $1.9 Billion
CEO			
1988 Bonus	30%	33%	37%
Salary	$265,000	$321,000	$431,000
Second Highest			
1988 Bonus	27%	32%	41%
Salary	$175,000	$210,000	$280,000
Third Highest			
1988 Bonus	26%	31%	38%
Salary	$137,000	$168,000	$229,000
Fourth Highest			
1988 Bonus	24%	28%	35%
Salary	$119,000	$146,000	$199,000
Fifth Highest			
1988 Bonus	23%	27%	33%
Salary	$106,000	$131,000	$182,000

Table 156: 1988 Bonus Awards

1988 Bonus Awards (Percent of Salary)	CEOS		Second Highest Paid		Third Highest Paid		Fourth Highest Paid		Fifth Highest Paid	
	Number	Percent	Number	Percent	Number	Percent	Number	Percent	Number	Percent
70 or more	3	7%	5	11%	3	7%	3	7%	1	2%
50-59	9	20	11	25	7	15	6	13	5	11
40-49	10	23	7	16	11	24	9	20	9	20
30-39	6	14	4	9	5	11	9	20	8	18
20-29	7	16	8	18	8	17	4	9	11	24
10-19	6	14	6	14	7	15	11	24	8	18
Less than 10%	3	7	3	7	5	11	3	7	3	7
Total	44	100%	44	100%	46	100%	45	100%	45	100%
Median Bonus	38%		40%		34%		36%		30%	
Middle 50% Range	22 – 51%		22 – 50%		14 – 48%		18 – 47%		20 – 45%	

Chart 19: Total Current Compensation of the Five Highest-Paid Executives, by Premium Income

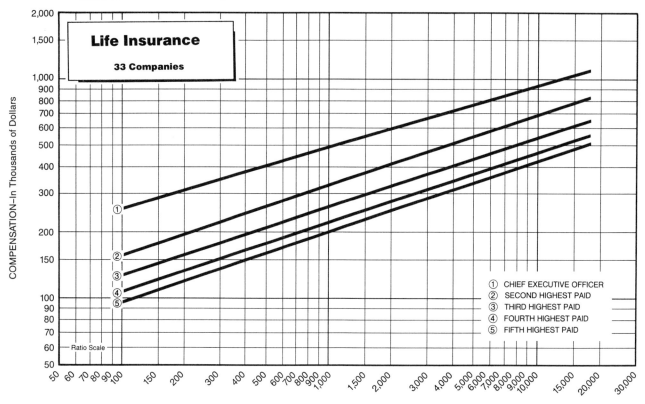

TOTAL PREMIUM INCOME–In Millions of Dollars

Table 157: 1988 Premium Income

	Companies	
1988 Premium Income	Number	Percent
$5 billion and over	4	12%
2-4,999 billion	4	12
1-1,999 billion	7	21
500-999 million	4	12
300-499 million	6	18
200-299 million	3	9
199 million and under	5	15
Total	33	100%

	Middle 50% Range	
Median	Low	High
$886 million	$307 million	$1.9 billion

Table 158: 1988 Total Current Compensation Regression Formula

Compensation Rank	Formula	r^2
CEO	log Y = 1.8290 + 0.2840 log X	43%
Second highest	log Y = 1.5840 + 0.3110 log X	46
Third highest	log Y = 1.4530 + 0.3210 log X	51
Fourth highest	log Y = 1.3750 + 0.3230 log X	59
Fifth highest	log Y = 1.3410 + 0.3200 log X	61

Table 159: 1988 Salary Regression Formula

Compensation Rank	Formula	r^2
CEO	log Y = 1.8550 + 0.2400 log X	46%
Second highest	log Y = 1.6980 + 0.2340 log X	39
Third highest	log Y = 1.5730 + 0.2430 log X	48
Fourth highest	log Y = 1.4600 + 0.2590 log X	62
Fifth highest	log Y = 1.4340 + 0.2570 log X	58

Chart 20: Total Current Compensation of the Five Highest-Paid Executives, by Premium Income

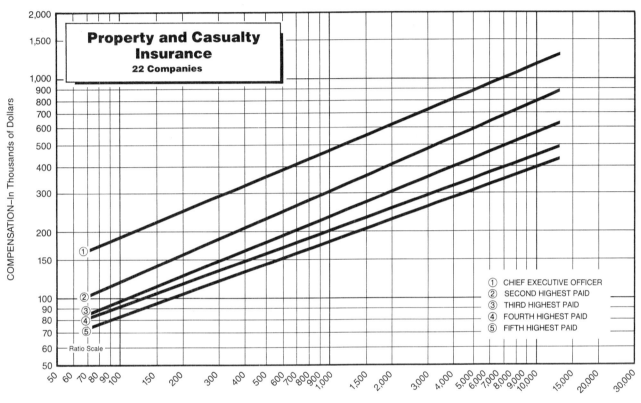

TOTAL PREMIUM INCOME–In Millions of Dollars

Table 160: 1988 Premium Income

	Companies	
1988 Premium Income	Number	Percent
$5 billion and over	3	14%
2-4,999 billion	2	9
1-1,999 billion	1	5
500-999 million	5	23
300-499 million	4	18
200-299 million	1	5
199 million and under	6	27
Total	22	100%

	Middle 50% Range	
Median	Low	High
$435 million	$194 million	$1.0 billion

Table 161: 1988 Total Current Compensation Regression Formula

Compensation Rank	Formula	r^2
CEO	log Y = 1.4910 + 0.3920 log X	79%
Second highest	log Y = 1.2170 + 0.4200 log X	84
Third highest	log Y = 1.1940 + 0.3900 log X	84
Fourth highest	log Y = 1.2690 + 0.3450 log X	83
Fifth highest	log Y = 1.2260 + 0.3420 log X	88

Table 162: 1988 Salary Regression Formula

Compensation Rank	Formula	r^2
CEO	log Y = 1.4530 + 0.3660 log X	83%
Second highest	log Y = 1.2130 + 0.3840 log X	82
Third highest	log Y = 1.1260 + 0.3810 log X	88
Fourth highest	log Y = 1.2530 + 0.3170 log X	86
Fifth highest	log Y = 1.2000 + 0.3190 log X	89

Chapter 11
Trade

Chart 21: Total Current Compensation of the Five Highest-Paid Executives, by Company Sales

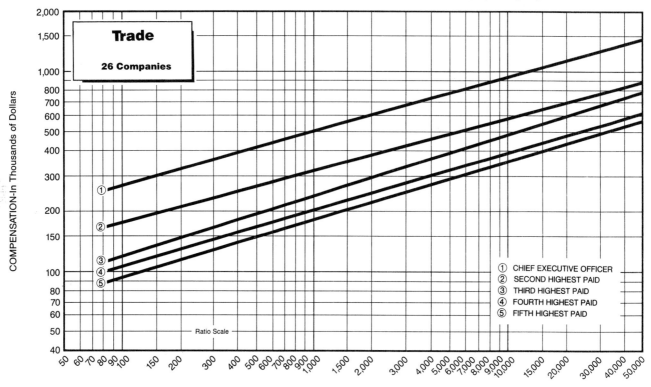

SALES-In Millions of Dollars

Table 163: 1988 Sales Volume

1988 Sales	Companies	
	Number	Percent
$5 billion and over	10	38%
2-4,999 billion	1	4
1-1,999 billion	5	19
500-999 million	4	15
300-499 million	4	15
200-299 million	—	—
199 million and under	2	8
Total	26	100%

Median	Middle 50% Range	
	Low	High
$1.4 billion	$555 million	$6.9 billion

Table 164: 1988 Total Current Compensation

Compensation Rank	Median	Middle 50% Range	
		Low	High
CEO	$621,000	$375,000	$1,000,000
Second highest	394,000	268,000	594,000
Third highest	297,000	198,000	560,000
Fourth highest	206,000	174,000	405,000
Fifth highest	187,000	148,000	320,000

Table 165: 1988 Total Current Compensation Regression Formula

Compensation Rank	Formula	r^2
CEO	$\log Y = 1.8980 + 0.2660 \log X$	59%
Second highest	$\log Y = 1.7250 + 0.2600 \log X$	60
Third highest	$\log Y = 1.4850 + 0.2990 \log X$	65
Fourth highest	$\log Y = 1.4310 + 0.2970 \log X$	65
Fifth highest	$\log Y = 1.3720 + 0.2950 \log X$	69

Table 166: Total Current Compensation as a Percentage of CEO's Total Current Compensation

Compensation Rank	Median	Middle 50% Range Low	High
Second highest	69%	58%	80%
Third highest	53	46	58
Fourth highest	44	39	56
Fifth highest	37	32	47

Table 167: 1988 Salary

Compensation Rank	Median	Middle 50% Range Low	High
CEO	$350,000	$275,000	$700,000
Second highest	265,000	208,000	300,000
Third highest	196,000	140,000	284,000
Fourth highest	161,000	126,000	251,000
Fifth highest	148,000	115,000	235,000

Table 168: 1988 Salary Regression Formula

Compensation Rank	Formula	r^2
CEO	$\log Y = 1.6600 + 0.2870 \log X$	68%
Second highest	$\log Y = 1.4340 + 0.2910 \log X$	72
Third highest	$\log Y = 1.2930 + 0.2860 \log X$	60
Fourth highest	$\log Y = 1.1910 + 0.3080 \log X$	84
Fifth highest	$\log Y = 1.1210 + 0.3170 \log X$	71

Table 169: Salary as a Percentage of CEO's Salary

Compensation Rank	Median	Middle 50% Range Low	High
Second highest	74%	55%	83%
Third highest	53	49	60
Fourth highest	49	43	53
Fifth highest	42	37	50

Table 170: 1988 Bonus Awards (as Percent of Salary), by Company Size

Executive	Sales Volume Middle 50% Range Low $555 Million	Median $1.4 Billion	High $6.9 Billion
CEO			
1988 Bonus	57%	56%	55%
Salary	$294,000	$365,000	$531,000
Second Highest			
1988 Bonus	39%	42%	48%
Salary	$218,000	$258,000	$345,000
Third Highest			
1988 Bonus	35%	40%	49%
Salary	$161,000	$198,000	$282,000
Fourth Highest			
1988 Bonus	31%	34%	39%
Salary	$141,000	$178,000	$265,000
Fifth Highest			
1988 Bonus	29%	30%	34%
Salary	$123,000	$156,000	$233,000

Table 171: 1988 Bonus Awards

1988 Bonus Awards (Percent of Salary)	CEOS		Second Highest Paid		Third Highest Paid		Fourth Highest Paid		Fifth Highest Paid	
	Number	Percent	Number	Percent	Number	Percent	Number	Percent	Number	Percent
100% or more	2	9%	3	14%	1	5	—	—	—	—
70-99	2	9	1	5	3	14	1	5%	1	5%
50-69	5	23	4	19	4	18	3	14	2	10
40-49	5	23	2	10	2	9	7	33	6	30
30-39	3	14	4	19	7	32	4	19	3	15
20-29	4	18	5	24	2	9	4	19	6	30
Less than 20%	1	5	2	10	3	14	2	10	2	10
Total	22	100%	21	100%	22	100%	21	100%	20	100%
Median Bonus	45%		39%		36%		40%		34%	
Middle 50% Range	30 – 66%		24 – 57%		31 – 60%		27 – 44%		26 – 41%	

Chapter 12
Utilities

Chart 22: Total Current Compensation of the Five Highest-Paid Executives, by Operating Revenue

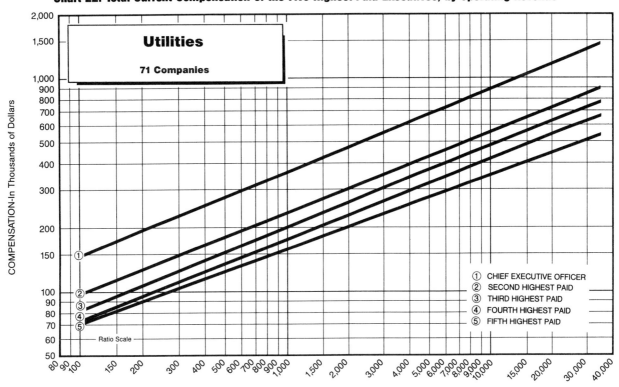

OPERATING REVENUE—In Millions of Dollars

Legend:
① CHIEF EXECUTIVE OFFICER
② SECOND HIGHEST PAID
③ THIRD HIGHEST PAID
④ FOURTH HIGHEST PAID
⑤ FIFTH HIGHEST PAID

Utilities
71 Companies

COMPENSATION-In Thousands of Dollars

Ratio Scale

Table 172: 1988 Operating Revenue

1988 Operating Revenue	Companies	
	Number	Percent
$5 billion and over	11	15%
2-4,999 billion	16	23
1-1,999 billion	12	17
500-999 million	12	17
300-499 million	11	15
200-299 million	4	6
199 million and under	5	7
Total	71	100%

Median	Middle 50% Range	
	Low	High
$1.1 billion	$477 million	$3.1 billion

Table 173: 1988 Total Current Compensation

Compensation Rank	Median	Middle 50% Range	
		Low	High
CEO	$357,000	$259,000	$610,000
Second highest	257,000	161,000	373,000
Third highest	200,000	138,000	316,000
Fourth highest	181,000	115,000	257,000
Fifth highest	156,000	123,000	219,000

Table 174: 1988 Total Current Compensation Regression Formula

Compensation Rank	Formula	r^2
CEO	$\log Y = 1.3990 + 0.3880 \log X$	70%
Second highest	$\log Y = 1.2300 + 0.3780 \log X$	72
Third highest	$\log Y = 1.1310 + 0.3870 \log X$	71
Fourth highest	$\log Y = 1.1260 + 0.3710 \log X$	72
Fifth highest	$\log Y = 1.1830 + 0.3370 \log X$	67

Table 175: Total Current Compensation as a Percentage of CEO's Total Current Compensation

Compensation Rank	Median	Middle 50% Range Low	Middle 50% Range High
Second highest	65%	57%	69%
Third highest	53	47	61
Fourth highest	47	42	54
Fifth highest	42	38	48

Table 176: 1988 Salary

Compensation Rank	Median	Middle 50% Range Low	Middle 50% Range High
CEO	$315,000	$230,000	$455,000
Second highest	205,000	149,000	297,000
Third highest	175,000	120,000	257,000
Fourth highest	158,000	110,000	225,000
Fifth highest	145,000	104,000	180,000

Table 177: 1988 Salary Regression Formula

Compensation Rank	Formula	r^2
CEO	$\log Y = 1.5600 + 0.3060 \log X$	77%
Second highest	$\log Y = 1.3460 + 0.3130 \log X$	80
Third highest	$\log Y = 1.2690 + 0.3170 \log X$	76
Fourth highest	$\log Y = 1.2470 + 0.3100 \log X$	77
Fifth highest	$\log Y = 1.2950 + 0.2810 \log X$	71

Table 178: Salary as a Percentage of CEO's Salary

Compensation Rank	Median	Middle 50% Range Low	Middle 50% Range High
Second highest	67%	57%	71%
Third highest	55	48	60
Fourth highest	49	44	61
Fifth highest	46	42	51

Table 179: 1988 Bonus Awards (as Percent of Salary), by Company Size

Executive	Operating Revenue Middle 50% Range Low $477 Million	Operating Revenue Middle 50% Range Median $1.1 Billion	Operating Revenue Middle 50% Range High $3.1 Billion
CEO			
1988 Bonus	28%	36%	48%
Salary	$257,000	$324,000	$432,000
Second Highest			
1988 Bonus	27%	33%	40%
Salary	$162,000	$207,000	$280,000
Third Highest			
1988 Bonus	24%	31%	40%
Salary	$139,000	$179,000	$245,000
Fourth Highest			
1988 Bonus	20%	25%	33%
Salary	$126,000	$162,000	$223,000
Fifth Highest			
1988 Bonus	18%	24%	31%
Salary	$118,000	$149,000	$198,000

Table 180: 1988 Bonus Awards

1988 Bonus Awards (Percent of Salary)	CEOS		Second Highest Paid		Third Highest Paid		Fourth Highest Paid		Fifth Highest Paid	
	Number	Percent	Number	Percent	Number	Percent	Number	Percent	Number	Percent
100% or more	2	5%	—	—	—	—	—	—	—	—
80-99	6	14	3	7%	1	2%	2	5%	2	5%
60-79	2	5	5	11	4	9	4	9	3	7
50-59	4	9	3	7	6	14	4	9	3	7
40-49	5	12	4	9	6	14	2	5	4	10
30-39	8	19	11	24	9	21	4	9	3	7
20-29	8	19	9	20	8	19	8	19	8	20
10-19	6	14	8	18	8	19	13	30	14	34
Less than 10%	2	5	2	4	1	2	6	14	4	10
Total	43	100%	45	100%	43	100%	43	100%	41	100%
Median Bonus	36%		32%		33%		24%		23%	
Middle 50% Range	20 – 59%		21 – 49%		21 – 50%		15 – 47%		15 – 44%	

Appendix
Procedure for Using Regression Equations

In the equations, X is total assets (commercial banking), premium income (insurance), operating revenue (utilities), or sales volume (all other industries). These are expressed in millions of dollars. That is, six zeroes are dropped. Y is total current compensation or salary expressed in thousands of dollars. That is, three zeroes are dropped. The "coefficient of determination" (r^2) is given in each formula. This is the ratio of the variation in total current compensation or salary explained by the regression line to the total variation in pay. (The square root of this coefficient is the correlation coefficient.) The logarithms are base ten.

Example:

Using the equaltion log Y = 1.7390 + 0.3.000 (log X), one can calculate the total current compensation of the chief executive in a company with sales of $500 million.

1. First set X = 500, that is, 500,000,000 with six zeroes dropped.

2. Log X = 2.6990
3. Multiply log X by 0.3000, which is the coefficient of the variable log X in the given equation. This results in a value of 0.8097.
4. Add to 0.8097 the constant in the equation, 1.7390. The result, 2.5487, is the value of log Y.
5. The chief executive's total current compensation is the antilog of log Y, which is 354. Read in thousands of dollars, it is $354,000.

Equation: log Y = 1.7390 + 0.3000 (log X)
   X = $500,000,000 = 500
   log X = 2.6990
   log Y = 1.7390 + 0.3000 (2.6990)
   log Y = 1.7390 + 0.8097
   log Y = 2.5487
   antilog Y = 354
   Y = $354,000